# Contents

# Substance Safety Information

# Foreward

Psychedelic drugs are helping people cure mental health problems such as addiction, and depression. Psychedelic drugs were once thought to have no value. Psilocybin mushrooms, LSD, and even cannabis, were demonized, and rejected. That is, until we started to face a mental health epidemic. Depression rates rising every year, and mental health problems are getting more and more common.

Canada became one of the first countries to take the lead with psychedelic medicine. The University of Toronto is home to one of the world's first reseach centers dedicated to studying how psychedelic drugs can improve our mental health. In the summer of 2020, four patients with incurable cancer were allowed to access to psilocybin meant to treat anxiety and depression related to their cancer diagnosis.

At least one other person was allowed to use psilocybin to treat long-standing depression issues by taking part in a similar treatment in November 2020. These patients are given purified psilocybin in a capsule, or pill, and they are carefully monitored by doctors while under the effects.

But not everyone will be able to access this model of psychedelic treatments. Psychedelics given by doctors in a controlled setting can be quite expensive for the patients to pay out of pocket. It's also not easy at all to find a reputable psychedelic guide. Which is why people are taking things one step further, and fighting for the right to use these drugs for their own long-term health and happiness.

Oregon became the first state in the USA to fully legalize psilocybin for therapeutic use. Oregon also decriminalized the possession of small amounts of all drugs for personal use. During their 2020 election, American voters decided to decriminalize the use of psychedelics in Washington DC, the capital city of the United States. Psychedelics have also been decriminalized for personal use in many other U.S. cities and counties such as Oakland, and Santa Cruz in California, as well as Denver in Colorado. Thirty-one states now allow adult use of cannabis in some form, while 33 other states allow medical cannabis use. Four out of five of inhabited US Territories have also allowed adult use in some form. The other being American Samoa, where cannabis remains illegal as of 2020.

In Europe, France has begun the process of changing some laws related to cannabis possession. Italy legalized medical cannabis in 2013, and allows the smoking of hemp products as of 2016, which shows a growing tolerance for cannabis use.

In Spain and the Netherlands, cannabis can be bought from specialized cafes. These cafes are left alone by law enforcement, but not actually legal. However they show a massive tolerance for the use and sale of cannabis in shops and storefronts.

The Netherlands also allows the use, and sale of psilocybin truffles. Which are similar to psilocybin mushrooms, because they contain psilocybin, but are in the form of a truffle instead of a traditional mushroom.

I do not encourage the use of drugs, psychedelic or otherwise. This book is meant to be used for harm reduction purposes. It is a source of information meant to educate the public on the historical and modern use of psychedelic drugs, plants, and fungi. As well as provide historical context for how ancient people made use of these powerful plants, and fungi. This way, we can show how psychedelics helped our ancestors, and how they can be used to help us today.

It is highly recommend that you practice meditation, yoga, or breathing exercises, like holotropic breathwork before even thinking about taking a psychedelic of any kind. Your body is already hard-wired to have a spiritual, and out-of-body experience. You do it in your sleep every night in your dreams, after all!

"If you get the message,
hang up the phone.
For psychedelic drugs
are simply instruments, like
microscopes, and telescopes, and
telephones.

The Biologist does not sit with
eye permanently glued to the
microscope, he goes away and
works on what he's seen,"

*– Alan Watts,*

*Author, philosopher.*

# An Introduction to Harm Reduction
## Let's talk openly about psychedelic drugs

People use drugs. Most of the world allows the sale of drugs such as alcohol and tobacco. But these two drugs are among the most toxic, and potentially dangerous substances on earth. Meanwhile, psychedelic drugs like LSD, cannabis, and psilocybin mushrooms are not tolerated by law enforcement in most of the world. In response to the unfair demonization of drugs, Ethnobotanist, and author Terence McKenna once said,

"Psychedelics are illegal not because a loving government is concerned that you may jump out of a third story window. Psychedelics are illegal because they dissolve opinion structures and culturally laid down models of behaviour and information processing,"

We were all told many lies about drugs, and the people that use them. We need to overcome the wrongfully held belief that drug use is wrong.

Drug use is a natural human impulse, like hunger or sexuality. We are driven to alter our minds in one way or another. The desire to alter our brainwaves is part of the human experience whether it's through caffeine, television, ketamine, LSD, weed, or deep breathing.

That being said, we need to teach people who use drugs how to keep themselves alive, it's that simple. If regulating the most toxic substances works to protect, and inform the vast majority of people who use them, then why not regulate the sale of more than just beer and cigarettes.

The general public is aware of how to use tobacco and alcohol responsibly. Even though alcohol is responsible for the death of five percent of drinkers annually, that's one in 20 people. Alcohol related deaths were close to three million in 2016. That's the equivalent of the population of Jamaica dying every single year because of a beverage we think is tasty.

Alcohol is known to cause addiction, death, overdose, aggressive behavior. These are all things that drugs like cannabis simply do not cause. But despite all this we still encourage people to be educated, and drink responsibly. Tobacco is another example of a drug that is known to cause cancer, and even kill millions of users every year. But cigarettes are still sold at every corner store, as long as they have warning labels that tell you the risks of smoking.

Why? Because we give people the right to choose for themselves. Because we can not tell others how to treat their bodies.

The same needs to be true of all other drugs. Drugs like Psilocybin mushrooms, and DMT (dimethyltriptamine) can help people who suffer from depression, end of life anxiety, eating disorders, and PTSD.

These, along with many other psychedelic drugs like LSD, MDMA, and cannabis have been proven to give people a spiritual-type experience, under the right circumstances.

In the ancient world, psychedelics held special, spiritual power. The ancient Greeks used a plant-based psychedelic wine every year to celebrate the fall harvest. Cannabis was one of the earliest medicines known to humanity, and hemp was the one of the most commonly used fabrics until the 20th century. There's even debate among experts that magic mushrooms could have played a major role in our evolution.

Psychedelics are, for the most part, physically safe. The overwhelming evidence says that psychedelics like LSD, and DMT can help people change their lives for the better. It then seems foolish at best to keep these drugs illegal. If magic mushrooms can cure PTSD, then it's time to take a new look at these drugs. As well as how we can make use of a history of psychedelic knowledge.

It's impossible to say that "all drugs are bad". Instead, we need to look at the facts. Drugs need to be evauated on a case by case basis. But regardless of laws, there's no reason why we shouldn't be telling each other how to stay safe in any risky situation., that includes taking drugs. So please stay safe, no matter what you choose to do. Make sure to always test your drugs, and do your research.

"We are chemical systems.
I hate to break it to you folks,

but we are made of drugs.
That's why drugs work!"


- *Dennis McKenna,*
*Ethnopharmacologist, author*

# The Stoned Ape
## Early humans who ate magic mushrooms

Ancient humans were known to use mind bending drinks, and drugs. These ranged from cannabis, to opium, and plant based psychedelic drugs. That includes the LSD-like Kykeon potion used during the Eleusinian Mystery festival in ancient Greece.

In fact, our love for getting high is so deeply a part of being human that some scientists think that drugs have helped shape us into the humans we are today. By helping our brains grow new cells, mushrooms may have to survive.

The Stoned Ape is a hypothesis that suggests that psilocybin mushrooms, or magic mushrooms, could have been the reason that human brains nearly doubled in size and power over a short time in our evolution.

The idea was first thought of by Ethnobotanist Terence McKenna, and later adapted by his brother the pharmacologist and Ethnobotanist Dennis McKenna, and world famous mushroom scientist, Paul Stamets. Both Terrence, and Dennis pioneered the earliest ways to harvest magic mushrooms at home. This, along with decades of hard research about how psychedelics affect us, has had a major impact on the world of psychedelic drugs, and the knowledge we have about them today.

Psilocybin mushrooms often prefer to grow in the dung (poop) of wild grass eating animals. There are also a range of psilocybin mushrooms that grow on decomposing plant life.

The idea is that while early humans were hunting, they would have come across psilocybin mushrooms in the dung of those animals, or growing on decayed plants.

Our earliest ancestors may have eaten them too, by looking for grubs, or insects eating the dung left behind by these same wild grass-eaters. While searching for grubs, it's possible that they would have seen the mushrooms and eaten them all the same.

Early humans in tribes might have added these mushrooms to their diet for a few reasons. For one, small amounts of mushrooms could have helped in the hunting and gathering process. Micro-doses of mushrooms are

known to increase edge detection. Which means you can see things a little more clearly, like a wild animal in a dense forest, or a plant that's hard to spot.

"These magic mushrooms open up the amount of information you receive," said mycologist Paul Stamets.

He goes on to state that because the mushrooms tend to give users visions of geometric patterns and feelings of insight, that early humans could have used these new ideas given to them while high to better be able to survive.

"Wow, what a competitive advantage. Especially if you're working with the geometry of weapons, or having to put something together that will give you a better chance of survival." he adds.

Psilocybin has also been shown to increase emotional bonds in people. In other words, tripping on mushrooms can help you connect with your friends, family, and even strangers. This might have encouraged early humans to form relationships based on emotional bonds, and start tribes, and families. Some experts believe that psychedelic use of some kind was still common well into the medieval ages.

High doses of psychedelics like LSD, or psilocybin mushrooms can give users a spiritual-type experience. This has been proven by modern science to help cure trauma like PTSD, and even long-standing mental illness. It makes logical sense to think that early humans who ate a lot of mushrooms might have had the same emotionally healing, and spiritual psychedelic trips that we know of today.

Mycologist Paul Stamets, has been given reports from people using psilocybin mushrooms that they can increase your awareness of sound. This increased hearing has yet to be studied. But if it's true, it would have been a great benefit to early humans who used them. Which would be pretty helpful if you're trying to listen for a predator sneaking up on you, like a giant, hungry cat.

According to Paul Stamets, this systematic use of magic mushrooms was passed down by generations of early humans. Repeated countless times over hundreds of thousands years. This has helped us to evolve us into the big brained, tech-loving, people we are today.

The main argument against the stoned ape hypothesis is that there is no way it can be tested in a lab. But recent studies have shown that psychedelics like psilocybin mushrooms, LSD, and DMT can regrow brain cells. The process of growing new brain cells is called neurogenesis and it's giving experts reason to think that the stoned ape hypothesis might hold more truth to it than once thought. So, it's possible that our ancient ancestors were eating magic mushrooms in a semi-strategic way to enhance their life, and the lives of everyone around them.

"[Psilocybin is] safer than Reese's Pieces, so you can't kill yourself with it, you can't overdose. It's non-addictive. As a matter of fact, it's anti-addictive.

It's a very, very ancient, sacred compound that's been used for eons by many different cultures in Africa, South America, Australia, and Europe.

It dissolves boundaries of race and class."

— Kilindi Iyi,
Psychedelic researcher,
mycologist, martial artist.

# The Philosopher's Stoned!
## The Mysteries in Eleusis

The ancient Greeks loved wine. But not the table wine that we know today. The wine of ancient Greece would have been closer to a drug then regular wine. The ancient Greeks spiked their wine with plants and fungi that gave the wine a range of effects. These plants could add medicinal value to the wine, enhance the flavour, or in some cases induce a psychedelic or intoxicating experience.

Pharmakon is the ancient Greek word which best translates to "drugs". It's even the base for many english words today such as pharmacy, where we go to buy over-the-counter drugs, and pharmacology, the study of drugs. The Pharmakon was usually a mix of plant-drugs of some kind. but often was used as simple medicine depending on the plants used. Think of Pharmakon as an overall word, used for medicine as well as altered states of mind. In the ancient world, there was no clear line between medicine, and drugs that got you high.

There were many psychoactive plants, and fungi that the ancient Greeks had access to. Resin from plants like cannabis, opium, mugwort, belladonna, henbane, mandrake, hemlock, ergot (LSD), species of psilocybin mushrooms, and even wild grass, and root-bark that had DMT in them have been found in Greek ruins.

"At the core of the mystery religions was an immediate or mystical encounter with the divine involving an approach to death and a return to life," says Brian Muraresku in his book The Immortality Key.

These plant-drugs are suspected by many scholars and researchers to be what caused these immediate or mystical encounters with the divine.

"For the level of brilliance on display in the School of Athens, bloody sacrifices to imaginary gods on far flung hill tops wouldn't quite do the job. That's where the Mysteries of Eleusis came in, just one of many so called mystery religions that fascinated the meditaranean mind in the old days," says Muraresku.

The Eleusinian Mysteries were a festival where a psychedelic potion with LSD-like effects called the Kykeon was used. Many famous people of the ancient world went to Eleusis to drink the potion, like Plato and Aristotle, Two of the most well-known philosophers in history.

Aristotle:

384BCE -322BCE

Philosopher from
Ancient Greece

Eventually, the rich were not the only ones who could access the Kykeon potion from the Eleusinian Mysteries. Normal people began creating their own rituals in their homes, instead of having to endure the long trip to Eleusis.

Philosphers like Plato, and Aristotle spoke of the experience of dying before you die. Which seems strange, and cryptic. But it may have been the best way they could describe what was happening to thier minds while on a psychedelic trip.

Psychedelics can bring on a feeling known as ego death, or ego dissolution. This can be described as a melting of your sense of self, or personal identity. It can also make you feel as if you are "one" with everything, or in tune with the world.

"Those inquisitive, cynical Greeks were looking for bona-fide evidence. Proof of the here-after. They would never blindly settle for empty promises of a future life among the heavens, they had to peak behind the curtain to see for themselves if there was any truth to the matter. For them and for us, how can religion be anything less?" continues Muraresku, speaking about the Eleusinian Mysteries.

The Eleusinian Mysteries began as a way to honour the goddess of the grain harvest. Demeter's [Deh-mitt-er] daughter Persephone, [Per-seh-fuh-knee] because it re-created the journey made by Demeter to find Persephone in the underworld in Greek religion.

For context, Persephone was taken by force to the "underworld". There are endless interpretations to the story, and what happened. But what's important to know is that Persephone was stuck in the "underworld", and her mother, Demeter, was going to find her one way or another.

Demeter searched and searched but had no luck. She

eventually came to the Greek city of Eleusis. This is where Demeter, disguised as an old woman, asks a man named Triptolemos for shelter. He offers to help her, and to repay him for his kindness, Demeter chooses to reveal the "secrets of agriculture" to him.

Triptolemos traveled all over the ancient greek empire teaching people from all over the "secrets of agriculture".

Many carvings, and reliefs of Triptolemos are found in ancient Greek ruins, including Italy, and as far west as Spain show him teaching other people how to use this potion.

This set of teachings is what gave rise to the Eleusinian Mysteries, a yearly festival meant to honour Demeter as she tried to find her daughter, Persephone. It was also to thank Demeter for teaching Triptolemos, and therefore humanity the "secrets of agriculture".

Triptolemos taught the "secret of agriculture" to anyone who wanted to learn. Once his students had learned the secrets, they would be given a long staff called a Thyrsos.

The thyrsos is a staff with a hollow tip, used to carry plant-drugs. It was also meant to symbolize their professional knowl-

(1) Persephone, Demeter, and Triptolemos at Eleusis. (Courtesy Napoleon Vier. Nov, 30, 2005)

edge. This is similar to how a degree or PhD would give a doctor authority in the medical field today.

But what were the "secrets of agriculture"? The ancient Greeks were a fairly advanced society for their time, having tackled mathematics, and philosophy. They already had farms to feed their cities, so why would the secrets of agriculture be worth their time? Wouldn't they have already known how to farm grain? Yes. They certainly did. But there's a lot of evidence to suggest that the "secrets of agriculture" were not meant to teach people to grow food, but rather how to create a psychedelic wine.

Brian Muraresku proposes that the "secrets of agriculture" were a set of instructions about how to properly handle grain that has been infected with ergot, a fungus that LSD can be derived.

The secrets would have instructed people how to control how much ergot grew on the grain without causing death, or ergotism, otherwise known as "St. Anthony's Fire". This was a real concern if you were making a psychedelic drink, using ergot. Ergotism is a serious disease, and can even cause death. Which may be why the "secrets of agriculture" were so respected in the time of the ancient Greeks.

Historically, cases of St. Anthony's Fire could be deadly, and infect thousands of people. This was because the Ergot fungus that caused the disease grows on grains like wheat and barley. In the year 994 C.E. the people of France witnessed between 20,000 and 40,000 deaths caused by St. Anthony's Fire. Ergotism has a range of awful symptoms such as gangrene, convulsions, sores and hallucinations. But if the ergot was handled carefully, it may have been the reason that people travelled to Eleusis to experience the Mysteries first hand.

The trek from Athens to Eleusis is about 32 kilometers, a six-and-a-half-hour walk, according to Google Maps. The end goal of the long journey was to honour the goddess Demeter, and her Daughter Persephone. It's almost impossible that the Greeks were not having some kind of drug experience during the festival in Eleusis.

People travelled from all over the Greek empire, not just from Athens. This makes it natural to think that the people who attended the festival at Eleusis did something memorable as a way to celebrate their religious beliefs, and mark the occaision.

Using psychedelic, or plant based drugs to have a religious, or spiritual experience has survived and thrived into the 21st century. The modern wave of doctors using psychedelic

### Ergot:

a potentially toxic fungus that grows on wheat. It may have been a central part of religious ceremonies, and yearly festivals because it has effects closely related to LSD.

medicine to treat the mentall ill is in full swing. With experiences involving psychedelics like MDMA, psilocybin, and ketamine helping people find meaning in their lives.

Making pilgrimages to far off places to use psychedelics seems to have stuck around too. Some people make trips across the globe to experience a psychedelic ceremony in a traditional setting.

We know now, thanks to research done by Johns Hopkins University, and many more. We know that psychedelics like psilocybin, and LSD can create a mystical-type experience. Simillar to those achieved by skilled meditators.

Every year, tourists travel to the Amazon Rainforest, and the mountains of Mexico to have a ceremony using psychedelics like psilocybin mushrooms, peyote, ayahuasca, or iboga. Much like the ancient Greeks who took part in the Eleusinian Mysteries, we are making our own journeys to have our own psychedelic experiences and experience the divine once more.

"Taking LSD was
a profound experience.

One of the most important
things in my life,"

- Steve Jobs,
Founder of Apple, CEO.

# The History of Cannabis
## Humanity's love affair with weed

Cannabis has been considered a "sacred" herb for thousands of years. Many cultures have used cannabis in one way or another for religious ceremonies. in some parts of the world, early Christians may have been exposed to cannabis smoke from the scented smoke from the censer, the incense burner swung by Christian priests.

The earliest known person to heal people with cannabis was Shennong, the ancient Chinese medicine man. "Shennong" can be translated to mean "divine farmer" "agriculture god" depending on the interpretation.

Shennong was an expert botanist, meaning he was the first known person to study the effects of herbal drugs on the human body. According to stories about him, Shennong wore clothing made of wild medicinal plants. He would also chew on the stems of various plants to test out what effects they had on him. He would use this knowledge from self-experimenting with the herbal drugs around him to heal other people.

A study published in the journal Science Advances, in June 2019 found remains of cannabis that would have been burned as a part of a funeral ceremony in ancient China.

"This phytochemical analysis indicates that cannabis plants were burned in wooden braziers during mortuary ceremonies at the Jirzankal Cemetery (ca. 500 BCE) in the eastern Pamirs region. This suggests cannabis was smoked as part of ritual and/or religious activities in western China by at least 2500 years ago and that the cannabis plants produced high levels of psychoactive compounds," as the study says.

The study goes on to state that there is still "a largely unanswered question as to when, where, and how the plant was first cultivated for higher psychoactive tetrahydrocannabinol (THC) production,"

This means that the origin of cannabis that could get it's users "high" is still unknown. What is known however, is that ancient people would have used cannabis for many reasons, including medicine and making fabric. It's also well known that humans would have brought cannabis with them everywhere they went, because of its many different uses.

Archaeologists have also found cannabis resin inside an ancient temple in southern Israel which dates back to the 8th-century B.C.E. Another study published in the April 2018 issue of Science, explores how psychoactive plants such as cannabis would have been used in the ancient Middle East (Anatolia Egypt, Mesopotamia, Sumer, etc).

"For as long as there has been civilization, there have been mind-altering drugs. Alcohol has been around for at least 10,000 years, but recent advances in chemical analysis of old pots reveal that other psychoactive drugs were present at the dawn of the first complex societies some 5000 years ago in the ancient Middle East. Ancient people from Turkey to Egypt experimented with local substances such as blue water lily, while imports like cannabis and opium made from poppies spread through early international trade networks. Armed with the new data, archaeologists are probing just how these drugs impacted early societies and beliefs. Some argue that the impact of these psychoactive substances has been underestimated, and that a drug culture was central to ritual in Mesopotamia, Anatolia, Egypt, and the Levant." adds the study.

The non-psychoactive version of the cannabis plant, hemp, was used to make fabric, construction, and food. A study published by MIT in the year 2000 found that hemp was highly praised, and it was farmed on a world-wide scale for many thousands of years.

Hemp was probably the earliest plant cultivated for textile fiber. Archaeologists found a remnant of hemp cloth in ancient Mesopotamia (currently Iran and Iraq) which dates back to 8,000 BC. Hemp is also believed to be the oldest example of human industry. In the Lu Shi, a Chinese work of the Sung dynasty (500 AD), we find reference to the Emperor Shen Nung (28th century BC) who taught his people to cultivate hemp for cloth. It is believed that hemp made it to Europe in approximately 1,200 BC. From there, it spread throughout the ancient world

China has the longest history of farming hemp, going back over six thousand years. Other countries like Chile, Spain, France, and Russia have records of farming hemp that go back several hundred years.

In 2008 a study from the Journal of Experimental Botany, took a close look at a stash of weed that dates back to 700 B.C.E. The weed was buried at the Yanghai Tombs near Turpan, in the Xinjiang province of China. It was buried with a shaman, who is believed to have used his stash to get high, and commune with the spiritual world. The cannabis was in surprisingly good condition (for weed that was thousands of years old). According to the study, Cannabis in ancient China would have been used "as a medicinal or psychoactive agent, or an aid to divination."

Hemp was often the strongest fabric available, and therefore a great choice for making long-lasting clothes for ancient human societies. The English word for canvas, comes from the word cannabis. This may be in part because of its common use in making sails for the large trading ships of medieval Europe. Sails made using hemp were about three times stronger than the sails made from a cotton blend. Making them the better choice for large ships crossing the ocean. Hemp was so important that in 1535, King Henry the Eighth passed a law that required all farmers to grow hemp on their farms, on top of their existing crops. Failure to do so could be grounds for legal punishment.

Even into the 20th century, hemp was still a valuable resource. In the 1920's about 80% of clothing was still made using hemp. It was so cheap to produce hemp, that it became the next "billion-dollar crop".

Propaganda about marijuana was on the rise. Smoking weed in the early 20th century was not common. It was popular among minority groups, like black Americans, and Mexicans at the time. It was also well known in the jazz community which created a variety of slang words for cannabis to be able to discuss it in song lyrics, and in public. (i.e. Reefer, mary-jane, grass, jazz cigarettes, etc).

Harry Anslinger was the Commissioner for the Bureau of Narcotics at the time of alcohol prohibition. He was a deeply racist, and intolerant person. One of, if not the most famous example of his racism was his personal vandetta against Billie Holiday, a black woman who made a name for herself as a famous jazz singer. Sending her threats to her from the Bureau of Narcotics. This was not

out of the ordinary. Jazz clubs were often targetted because of their association to cannabis, and different cultures.

Anslinger used marijuana as a scare tactic to make
the public fear hispanic, and black Americans. Cannabis
was made illegal by 1933. He thought that by making weed
illegal, it would give the US government the right to break
down doors, and arrest people who they did not like.

This hurt the hemp industry. The fear of cannabis,
and immigrants had convinced the public that cannabis
was some kind of killer drug. The harvest of one of the
most valuable, useful plants on earth stopped almost overnight.

A paragraph in the MIT study comments that
"Hemp has been one of the most significant crops for
mankind up until this last century. It is astonishing to see
how the widespread use of hemp has been deteriorated to
such an extent that people barely recognise it as anything
but a plant that gets you high."

In October 2018, after nearly a century of criminal
penalties, arrests, false information about weed, Canada
chose to legalize it. Legal adults can now buy cannabis.

In 2020 the world has a very divided outlook on
weed. Many countries have laws that allow you to use
weed for personal reasons, like Jamaica, and of course,
The Netherlands. Amsterdam Coffee shops in the Netherlands have famously allowed the sale of cannabis up to
5 grams since the 1970's. This has created a sort of grey
area in the law, where cannabis is illegal, but tolerated by
police.

Medical cannabis dispensaries continue to provide cannabis to people with certain conditions. While in many American states, and in Canada medical cannabis is legal, in other places it can fall into a strange legal grey area much like the coffeeshops of Amsterdam. Meaning that you can get a prescription to use cannabis in theory, but using weed at all is still a crime. Or it could be entirely illegal depending on where you live.

Cannabis has been legal in Canada since 2018, and we see how regulating the sale of weed benefits everybody. Between April 2019, and March 2020 cannabis made 32 million dollars in tax revenue that could be used to fix hospitals, build schools, and help everyone deal with a global pandemic.

Hopefully the move to legalize cannabis will set an example for other countries around the world to follow. People need cannabis, for medicine, and for industry. More importantly, no one has the right to tell you what to do with your own body.

Getting high is your right as a human being, just like having access to medicine and clothing, shelter, and food. Cannabis has been giving us all these things for thousands of years, and might continue to do so for thousands of years to come.

# Can Psychedelics be Medication?
## What's behind a microdose

Psychedelic drugs are becoming available as a long-term treatment for a variety of mental health and physical problems.

Small doses of psychedelics are now being studied as an alternative to traditional anti-depression and anti-anxiety medication.

These small doses are called micro-doses, and have no psychedelic effects like visual distortions or funny sensations. A microdose can range from 10 to 20 percent of a recreational or psychedelic dose.

James Fadiman is a psychologist, author, and psychedelic researcher. He has spent decades researching meditation, as well as drugs like LSD and psilocybin mushrooms.

"When people are micro-dosing their positive emotions go up and their negative emotions decline," he said at the Science and Non-Duality conference in 2019.

He explains that while commonly used medications like anti-anxiety drugs tend to numb patients while making them able to tolerate being unhappy.

"Micro-doses work differently. They make you more able to be happy," He added.

Psychedelics were once the centerpiece of mental health research. During the 1950s's, an era of new discoveries, and potential cures was taking place. Cures for common problems like alcoholism, depression, and anxiety were within reach.

The general public began to hear about psychedelic drugs for the first time. And word of their benefit began to spread. It was understood that these were meant to be used by doctors, and researchers for the benefit of their patients. Others began to use them for self exploration, and meditation.

But in 1970, US President Richard Nixon signed the Controlled Substance Act, which made drugs like cannabis and psychedelics illegal. This caused all research into psychedelic drugs like LSD, psilocybin, and cannabis to come to a stop overnight in the United States.

Through international pressure, most countries around the world began adopting their own drug policies to keep up with the US.

In the years since, audio recordings have emerged in which President Nixon blamed various liberal and minority groups (to put it nicely) for the rise of youth drug use.

Even though research was hard to conduct during this time, it wasn't impossible. Small scale research was conducted on occasion. Groups like the Multidisciplinary Association for Psychedelic Studies have conducted research on MDMA, more commonly known as "ecstasy" for treatment of PTSD beginning in the mid-1980s.

In 2020, research into psychedelic drugs is officially booming again. People are begining to benefit from psychedelic medicine like microdosing.

This is partly due to the normalization of psychedelics by tech giants like Steve Jobs, sillicon valley programmers, and tens of thousands of people who attend psychedelic inspired events like Burning Man.

However, it's thanks to the tireless effort of researchers which has allowed psychedelic drugs to heal people once more.

# The Mysteries of Egypt
## Ancient plant chemistry

The ancient Egyptians had expert knowledge about how plants, and drugs, worked on the human body. Many traces of drugs like cannabis, and tobacco can be found in ancient Egyptian pottery, and mummified remains. These plant-drugs seem to have been important to the ancient Egyptians. An entire pharmacy of plant-drugs was available to the Egyptians. They could be used in religious rituals, or funerals, but also as medicine to treat the sick or injured. Sometimes even just to unwind at the end of the day, like we do today.

The drug of choice for most people in ancient Egyptian was the blue lotus, or blue water lily. It was steeped in beer, or wine to create a semi-psychedelic drink that would give the users a sedative-like high. The effects of blue lotus are well known today. This is because it has been used continuously by many cultures into the modern era. It now mostly is taken in tea, instead of wine.

The effects of cannabis are also well known. Cannabis, or weed is now one of the most commonly used drugs on earth. If these drugs were used by the ancient Egyptians, it would have given them the same effects that we see today in people who consume cannabis, or the blue lotus. So it's clear that the ancient Egyptians wanted to induce some kind of intoxication by using the plants available to them.

Weed was known to the Egyptians as both a medicine, and a mind altering drug. Cannabis pollen from around 3800 B.C.E. was found along the Nile Delta in Nagada, Egypt. A more convincing discovery was when cannabis pollen was also found in the mummified remains of Ramses II, who died in the year 1213 B.C.E.

The Goddess Seshat is usually shown with a five, or seven pointed symbol above her head. This is most likely a reference to a cannabis leaf. Suggesting that cannabis was somehow important in their religious beliefs.

According to research done by Lise Manniche, Author of "An Ancient Egyptian Herbal" as well as other modern-day Egyptologists, cannabis was referred to as "shum-shum-met" which litterally translates to "the medical marihuana plant".

Manniche identified several ancient egyptian documents that reference cannabis in some way. These include the Eber's Papyrus, Hearst Papyrus, and Berlin Papyrus. There are also well known ancient medical texts that describe cannabis and how to use it as medicine, such as the Chester-Beatty VI Papyrus.

The Egyptians also used these plant-drugs as a way to connect with the spirit world, or afterlife in a symbolic way. But strange signs of that suggest exactly this have been found in certain mummies. German toxicologist, Dr Svetla Balabanova found traces of nicotine and cocaine while examining mummified bodies in Manchester. She believes these drugs may have been used in the process of mummification.

This was thought to be a mistake at first. But analysis shows that cocaine and tobacco were really there, in the remains of the mummies. Lab tests, including GCMS (gas chromatography-mass spectrometry) tests proved time after time to be accurate.

"The first positive results, of course, were a shock for me. I had not expected to find nicotine and cocaine but that's what happened. I was absolutely sure it must be a mistake," says Dr. Balabanova.

Plants and drugs are usually only documented by the "one percent" of the ancient Egyptian world. Pharaohs, priests, and the wealthy were typically the only ones who wrote about their drug experiences. That doesn't mean that regular people didn't have access to them as well. But the evidence so far seems to show that only the rich were able to document what their drug use.

Cannabis, tobacco, cocaine, and blue lotus may have been a part of Egyptian life, and religious tradition in some way. But ancient Egypt had access to an entire pharmacy of plant-drugs. Not only that, these plants could certainly induce mystical experiences in the right conditions.

When looking for drugs in ancient Egyptian mythology, the Egyptian "Tree of Life" is a good place to start. The "Tree of Life" is believed to have been a species in the acacia family to contain significant amounts of DMT, and 5-MeO-DMT. Both of which are powerful psychedelic drugs.

Acacia Nilotica may also contain compounds similar to the MAOIs. Though further lab tests are needed to prove this. If it is true, it would suggest that Acacia Nilotica could have been taken by itself to induce an experience closely related to the ayahuasca experience. This, in theory could be similar to an ayahuasca, or psilocybin mushroom experience.

Psychologist and ethnobotanist Stephen R. Berlant believes that some of the crowns shown in ancient hieroglyphs are stylized representations of psilocybin mushrooms.

The "Hemhem" or "Triple Crown" is a ceremonial head-dress that looks very similar to a cluster of newly formed mushrooms. In some hieroglyphs, you can see the person wearing the triple crown is being fed an ankh. Debate over whether or not the ankh is also a stylized mushroom is ongoing.

The "White Crown" or "Hedjet" was worn by the rulers of Egypt. The White Crown also looks like a stylized baby mushroom, or "pin". This may have been a reference to the god Osiris, and the concept of rebirth as a whole.

If these are stylized mushrooms, it's natural to assume that they had some sort of drug-like effect (not just because they looked cool). It's also natural to assume that they may have been eaten in a religious ceremony, which would explain the big ceremonial crowns.

There are many examples of drugs like cannabis, and blue lotus being used in ancient Egyptian hieroglyphs. Therefore it's possible that they knew about, and even celebrated the ceremonial use of psilocybin mushrooms, or mushrooms that were otherwise psychoactive, like the Amanita Muscaria.

Until recent years, scientific fields of study did not usually share findings with each other, unless it was absolutely needed. But this has changed in recent years. Areas of study like chemistry, biology, and archaeology are working together like never before.

The goal is to use new technology, scientific methods, and reserch from different fields of study. Hopefully this will lead to new discoveries. One day, the secrets of ancient Egypt might eventually reveal themselves to the world, but for now they remain a mystery.

# Rat Park
## How addiction really works

What causes addiction? Drugs do right? Well, the answer is more complex than you'd expect.

Over 100 years of arresting people for using, and being addicted to drugs has led the world into an epidemic. Opiate use like heroin, and fentanyl is higher than ever. So what really causes addiction? What really makes people crave these drugs?

One of the most classic examples of drugs causing addiction is when a rat is placed in an empty cage by itself. The rat has only the option to drink water, or drink water laced with either heroin, or cocaine. Under these conditions, most of the time, the rat will choose to drink the drugged water until it dies.

But In the 1970's Professor Bruce Alexander decided to take another look at this experiment. He noticed that in this experiment, the rats had nothing that made their lives worth living. In other words, it was a rat's hell. No food, no toys, no entertainment, and no other rats to socialize and mate with.

So, the "Rat Park" experiment would put a group of rats in a cage together. They would have lots of food and water, and toys. They were also given the option of heroin or cocaine (depending on the test being done). The idea was to give the rats everything they could possibly need to be happy as they could be. This was what stopped addiction in its tracks.

Though the rats chose to use the drugs recreationally on rare occasions, none of them became addicted to the drugs. None of the rats used the drugged water on a regular basis. Professor Alexander began to realize that addiction isn't about the drugs, it was about the cage. In other words, addiction is an adaptation to having a life that is difficult to handle.

Drugs alone are not the reason people can become addicted. While drugs like heroin and cocaine have chemical hooks that can cause withdrawal effects, it's just not enough to cause addiction in anybody.

Drugs identical to heroin are used in hospitals to help manage pain during surgery. These are drugs like Morphine, and Oxycodone. They are powerful painkillers, and many people's lives have gotten better thanks to the use of these drugs by doctors.

But these drugs are also high purity, medical-grade drugs. This means that they're much stronger than the heroin bought on the street.

But the majority of people who were given Diamorphine, or morphine in a hospital never got addicted. Even when they were exposed to these powerful drugs.

"If your grandmother had a hip replacement, she didn't come out [of the surgery] as a junkie," As Johann Hari says in his Ted Talk on addiction.

"In rat park, they don't like the drugged water. They almost never use it. None of them ever use it compulsively. None of them ever overdose. You go from an almost 100%

45

overdose rate when they're isolated, to a 0% overdose rate when they have happy and connected lives." Hari added.

If you're thinking "Those are just rats not people." Then consider this, During the Vietnam war 20% of American soldiers were using heroin. The public was expecting a mass epidemic of addiction because of the heroin using soldiers returning home, and being "junkies" unable to do anything. This was not the case.

Much like rat park, the soldiers were using heroin because they were isolated, in a war zone. They also had access to drugs like heroin and cannabis while in Vietnam. This combination of being in an unhealthy situation, and having access to heroin, made them temporary addicts. Most of them simply stopped using any drugs as soon as they returned home, to the life they knew before the war.

We put people who are addicted to drugs in jail, tell them they are flawed, and that what they did was wrong. This is a backwards way of looking at addiction.

People who use drugs like cocaine and heroin need more support systems. Evidence shows that giving addicts and users a clean supply of drugs, and a support network of health-care workers can reduce overdose, and death in those who use drugs.

We also need to understand that addiction is what can happen when someone with a difficult life, and no emotional support is introduced to a temporary fix like hard drugs.

Portugal has had great success decriminalizing, and regulating the supply of drugs like heroin. In the 1990's one percent of Portugal's population was hooked on heroin, and the government realized that arresting users was not going to stop, or slow down the addiction epidemic.

Instead they decriminalized the use of all drugs for personal use. It's still illegal to deal drugs. But if you choose to use any drugs, the result is not a criminal record. It's often an introduction to rehabilitation programs which can help save lives.

"You're not alone, we love you," said Hari as a message to all addicts.

If you or someone you know struggles with addiction. The first step is to simply tell reach out and help them with their daily lives. The"Rat Park" experiments teach us a valuable lesson about how addiction works. Being connected to the people around you, and having meaning in your life can both prevent, and cure addiction.

"Fuck the Drug war. Dropping acid was a profound turning point for me, a seminal experience.

I make no apologies for it. More people should do acid. It should be sold over the counter,"

- George Carlin.
Stand-up comedian.

# What's a Testing Reagent?
## Drug Identification Kits

Drug testing may sound complicated, or confusing. But it's really easy! There are a number of websites that sell at-home drug test kits to identify many kinds of drugs. There are also test kits that check the purity of your drugs. To make sure it wasnt cut with anything else, some kits look for drugs like fentanyl, that may have somehow found their way into your stash.

Here's a quick guide to some of the drug ID test kits. Each kit identifies a certain type of drug. Test kits can be bought online. Simply searching up any of the kits listed below will give you many results. They are perfectly legal to buy in most countries.

## MANDELIN

&#x270F; Test for Identifying Ketamine.

&#x270F; It is also used as a secondary test to double check for MDMA and related drugs.

&#x270F; Methoxetamine (MXE) is often sold by dealers as ketamine.

&#x270F; Ketamine and MDMA are often cut with other drugs, like PMA so make sure to test each batch.

✐ Use this test to identify MDMA (Ecstacy, Molly, M)

✐ ID's many other drugs used to cut MDMA, like crystal meth (methamphetamine), heroin, and cocaine.

✐ Should always be used before taking "Ecstacy" (MDMA).

MARQUIS

---

EHRLICH

✐ Use this tests for drugs related to LSD, DMT, and Psilocybin (mushrooms).

✐ LSD, DMT, 5-MeO-DMT, AMT, 4-ACO-DMT, DIPT, 5-MeO-DIPT, and others.

---

✐ Use this test to identify opiates like heroin, morphine, codeine, oxycodone. As well as drugs that may contaminate the batch.

✐ It can also be used as another way to double check that MDMA was not mixed with drugs like DXM, a powerful cough medicine often sold as "Ecstacy".

MECKE

---

# Testing and Weighing
## your
## Plants, Powders, Pills, and Potions

Having a drug experience of any kind can be risky. All drugs, including psychedelics, stimulants, and alcohol present some kind of risk. But there are many steps you can take to make sure that everyone goes home happy and healthy.

Make sure the dose is right. The dose will always determine how intense the experience is going to be. When people use too much, it can be overwhelming. When people use too little it can sometimes lead to feeling restless, anxious, or uneasy.

Psychedelics like psilocybin, and LSD are very easy on your body. There are many cases of people taking hundreds, or even thousands of doses of LSD at once with little to no negative effects. But a psychedelic trip at any dose will affect how you think.

Even a calming experience at a low dose can lead you to question how you see things. You can start to examine your relationships with friends and family, and the world around you. So it's best to take some time to reflect on your trips. Check in with yourself the following day. Be nice, and go easy on yourself. In other words, make the next day a "me" day.

Keep in mind that the emotions brought up during a trip are only one side of the coin. Physical risks, such as overdose are a possibility when taking certain drugs. Psychedelics like MDMA (E, X, Molly, Ecstacy) and ketamine (K, Special K) have caused death in some by doing too much in one night, or by not following other safety guidelines.

These drugs are not dangerous on their own. But if the safety guidelines are ignored for some drugs, there are con-sqquences. Often MDMA pills bought on the street are dosed at two to three times the safe dose. Meaning that in some cases, when people buy a pressed powder pill of MDMA, they can be sold something much stronger than they wanted. This can lead to negative experiences, and if the users are not careful, death.

However death on MDMA is extremely rare, and only 2 in ten thousand new users ever die from complication. That's only 0.02% which is barely noticable compared to alcohol, which kills 1 in 20 people who drink, a rate of 5%. This made alcohol responsible for over 3 million deaths across the globe in 2016. A study done by professor David Nutt found that horseback riding caused a lot more deaths than MDMA does in the U.K.

When taking MDMA, it's important to stay hydrated. The body heat from things like moving around and dancing, combined with MDMA has caused cases of overheating.

With any drug, it's best to take half of your intended dose, and wait an hour before re-dosing. This can help you achieve the best experience, and stay safe.

With powdered drugs like DMT or ketamine, it's always best to use a test kit. There's simply no knowing what's in that off-white powder unless it's tested using a reagent kit.

Deaths can be sometimes be caused by using another drug by accident, like fentanyl which as found it's way into many other drugs ranging from heroin to cocaine, as well as in anonymous powders called "dope" by the people selling it. It's also worth noting that if someone tries to sell you "dope".

It's worth noting that those buying "dope" are usually not aware that "dope" it's not an actual substance. It can refer to any chemical, legal or illegal, that's put into a bag, and sold as a drug. It's best to stay far away from powders, or pills called "dope" because It's more than likely a mix of unwanted things that could be harmful.

Taking the wrong drug by accident is also a danger for those who use psychedelics like LSD. Research chemicals like 25i-Nbome are sometimes sold as "acid", and can be sometimes be deadly if the user if not careful.

If you plan on using any drug, wether it's cannabis, mushrooms, LSD, ketamine, or any other drug in the world, search what that drug does on the internet. Simply knowing what you are getting into can, and will save lives.

"[MDMA] takes away the feelings of self-hatred and condemnation, which are the biggest obstacles to insight,"

– Ann Shulgin.
Pioneer of psychedelic therapy, author.

# How to Make Hash
## the oldest cannabis extract

Hash is the oldest, and most well-known cannabis extract. Ancient remains of weed products have been found to be 2700 years old, and evidence suggests that it may have played a role in our early societies as a way to create medicine, as well as fabric for rope and cloth.

Smoking hash dates back to around the 1500s, when tobacco was introduced to Europe. Hash was mainly eaten until it regained popularity in the 20th century, and later with the beatnick, and hippie countercultureof the 1960's.

In the Victorian era Louisa May Alcott, the author of *Little Women,* was a fan of hash imported from India. Her story *Perilous Play* describes the experience of a group of young adults who decide to eat a bunch of hash candies to pass the time. Other authors of the time, like Fitz Hugh Ludlow also loved hash. His book "The Hasheesh Eater".

You can even find audiobook versions of both of these stories online. This is thanks to ethnobotanist Kathleen Harrison, and ethnobotanist and author Terence McKenna, who recorded the audio versions.

But in the 21st century, thanks to fancy weed smoking accessories, you can make your own hash without even leaving your house! But what exactly is it?

Hash, or hashish, is made by sifting and collecting the pollen of the cannabis plant. Commonly known as "kief" or "kif", it is heated and pressed. This pollen contains the cannabinoids of the plant. These cannabinoids contain the compounds that make weed medicinal, and psychoactive. Meaning that hash can be a more efficient way to consume cannabis, because it offers more bang for your buck, so to speak. It's also safe to produce yourself, assuming it's legal to do so in your country.

## Step 1: Gather some kief

This method will only make you a small, personal amount of hash from the kief you can collect from the bottom part of a 3-piece grinder. Kief can often be purchased at authorized cannabis vendors in places where cannabis is allowed, such as Canada and some U.S. states.

If you want to collect your own kief, you'll need some way to break down the cannabis, as well as a collection tray. This is why a 3-part grinder is perfect. This is because when you grind up the buds of weed, the kief will collect in the bottom of the grinder.

That being said, this step will take time if you choose to collect your own kief, but it will allow you to get the most out of your weed. Unless you already have a grinder full of kief, in which case, good job!

## Step 2: Parchment Paper

✳ Cut out a rectangular piece of parchment paper, and fold it in half. It should be big enough to put all of the kief into a pile on one half of the paper, with a lot of space around the edges.

✳ Carefully scrape or brush all of your kief onto the parchment paper.

✳ Now fold the other side over the kief and squish it with all your strength!

✳ You should now have a flat(ish) piece of kief between the folded parchment paper.

✳ Using a dab tool, paper clip, or toothpick works great for handling the kief pancake.

✳ Once that's done, remove the flap of paper and carefully fold the kief over itself.

✳ Repeat this process until you cannot squish the kief anymore.

## Step 3: Heating The Hash

🍁 You want to provide the kief with enough heat to cure, and turn a chocolate brown colour.

🍁 Boil some water over the stove. Using a pair of kitchen tongs, hold it over the steam for a few seconds, and give it another hard squish between your hands or under a heavy object like a rolling pin, or a book. (maybe even this book?)

🍁 Take your kitchen tongs and hold your kief over the boiling water for a few momments.

🍁 Remove it from the heat, and squish it again. Repeat this process a few more times until the kief becomes a darker brown colour.

## Step 4: Cool it down and enjoy!

✴ Let your new little hash chunk sit at room temperature for about 20 minutes, or until it's hard enough to manipulate with your bare hands without getting sticky.

✴ Then it should be ready to enjoy. Break it up and put in on top of a bowl, in a joint, or even with some tobacco. That's how easy it is!

   Hash is the oldest way to use cannabis extracts and it's probably the easiest to make yourself. No chemicals, just weed, somewhere to collect the kief that falls off the buds, and a little elbow grease.

"If the words 'life liberty and the pursuit of happiness' dont include the right to experiment with your own consciousness,

Then the Declaration of Independence isn't worth the hemp it was written on."


- *Terence McKenna,*

*Psychedelic researcher, athor.*

# Clandestine Psychedelica
## A ceremonial space for the modern world

The full moon shines through a large window onto a table with three decorative candle holders. The ones on the end are shaped like mushrooms, in the middle is a small stone Buddha holding a candle. Sitting in front of them is a small box of psilocybin mushrooms, commonly known as magic mushrooms. Small drums, crystals, and colourful figurines decorate shelves on the walls. Pillows, and blankets litter the floor. Four people prepare themselves to begin a clandestine psychedelic ceremony.

Many cultures have used psychedelic plants and fungi to reach altered states of consciousness. These altered states are used to heal emotional trauma. But they can also be used as tools for personal growth, and as tools for seeking out spiritual experiences.

"Some people go into a ceremony for healing. There is a sense that a ceremonial space will able to hold a healing experience for them. Ceremonies are usually attached to tradition, and tradition usually holds a context that will create a greater sense of safety for the participant to surrender and be guided through their experience," said James W. Jesso, author, public speaker, and expert on psychedelic culture.

According to the Global Drug Survey, most people who choose to have a psychedelic experience will do so alone, or with a small group of close friends. Many of these same people will also seek out a kind of guide, or shaman to help them through the experience.

"I have met psychiatrists and clinical psychologists who despite knowing they may be risking their careers, so value the addition of psychedelics to their work, that they offer such services as a side-line 'on the quiet'. I have met other people who have pitched up to a random venue, handed over their $200 and taken ayahuasca, along with 30 other people overseen by a 'neo-shaman'. Supervised psychedelic session are thus not a single entity," said Professor Adam R Winstock, a consultant psychiatrist and the director of the Global Drug Survey in 2019.

In Canada, psychedelic drugs are gaining attention as a breakthrough in mental health treatment. They show incredible promise for curing mental disorders that were previously thought to be incurable. Because of this, many cities and districts in the United States have decriminalized the personal use of psychedelics such as magic mushrooms, LSD, DMT, ayahuasca, and other plant psychedelics.

However, there is a lesser known, but thriving sub-culture that uses psychedelic plants to explore spiritual experiences. Since their introduction in the 1960s, psychedelic drugs have been used by spiritual seekers cross the globe.

During a Skype call in the spring of 2020, I had the pleasure to discuss with James how psychedelics are now being used in the in clandestine ceremonies for personal healing, and spiritual seeking.

"There's been an ongoing subculture of psychedelic therapy, as well as anecdotal reports of people being positively impacted since they arrived on the scene in the western world. There are ceremonies happening with lots of plant-type psychedelics, like ayahuasca, psilocybin mushrooms, peyote, or the San Pedro cactus," said Jesso.

Typically, a shaman guides participants through a ceremony. This is done by creating a controlled space, where people feel comfortable with each other, and with the guide.

"Any time someone is choosing to take a psychedelic, being in a context that is safe and where you are being cared for is beneficial. The more intense and disorienting the experience will be, the more important it is to have an experienced guide present," said Jesso.

However, the group was not planning to use a guide. There would be someone else present in case of an emergency. They were going to navigate the experience together.

"We admittedly don't have a shaman. But we also don't really need one. We don't really have shamans in our western society. So, I thought we should do it our own way. But we

should also acknowledge traditions that use psychedelics like psilocybin mushrooms. To try build off of them in a way that's relevant to us," said Terry, the host of that night's psilocybin ceremony. The group was confident about their decision.

"There was a strong sense of community among everyone who was there." said Jack, another member of the group.

Psychedelic-assisted therapy is seen as an effective treatment for a variety of mental illnesses. Experts are exploring how psychedelics, like psilocybin mushrooms, can treat people who suffer from mental health issues like depression, anxiety, and post traumatic stress disorder (PTSD). The Multidisciplinary Association for Psychedelic Studies (M.A.P.S.) has created a medical use of psychedelics based on traditional ceremonial settings. They do this by providing a quiet, supportive space with calming music, incense, and dim lighting, while the patient is guided by a trained therapist. By following this format, a patient's mental health can improve for several weeks after a single dose.

"Entering into a psychotherapists office is a type of ceremony. A ceremonial space is being opened, and a ceremonial space is being closed," said Jesso.

Psychedelics are used in this kind of setting because it allows users to examine how they see themselves, and how they live their daily lives.

"It's relaxing and therapeutic because it lets you think about your emotions and what's currently going on in your life," said Jack.

The ceremony begins, and the group consumes the psilocybin mushrooms. As the hours go by, each member of the group discusses what's on their mind while the others help them sort through their problems. Each member of the group is given a new and creative way to examine a situation. Each member supports the others through intense feelings. Each member is there for each other in a way that is rarely seen, or felt. Around midnight the effects wore off, and the group decides to go outside under the stars. The full moon is directly above them, and it's light sparkles on the freshly fallen snow.

"It was extremely therapeutic. It's something that a lot of people could use to improve their mental health. It can really help someone who's suffering during hard times," said Jack, a few days after the experience.

Whether it's in a doctor's office in the downtown, a shamanic retreat, or with people that you trust deeply, psychedelics are being used in secret all across the globe. The simple things can be easy to overlook, but they are often the most healing. Which means that sometimes the best medicine is having an experience that connects you to the world around you.

"If the doors of perception were cleansed, everything would appear to man as it truly is... Infinite.

For man has closed himself up, till he sees all things through a narrow chink of his cavern. "

- William Blake,
British poet, painter.

# How to Stay Safe:
## A harm reduction guide

The following pages contain information on using psychedelic drugs in a controlled, safe setting. This is not to encourage drug use. But it's important to present people with fact based information about the effects of all drugs. This way people will be able to weigh the risks or themselves.

Even though psychedelic drugs can give some people benefits under a doctor's watchful eye, going off on your own to have a drug experience of any kind can be risky. The risks are not always physical. The risks may not even not be related to the drug itself, but may arise from the setting, or the people you are with.

Make sure the dose is right. Dosing will make the difference between a relaxing time, and an intense, vivid experience. The dose always determines the experience. When people use more, or less of a substance than they intended, it can sometimes lead to anxiety.

Sometimes it's no big deal in the long term. Like eating a cannabis edible that was too strong. Other times, it can be the difference between a good time, and a bad time.

Psychedelics like psilocybin, and LSD are very easy on your body. There are many cases of people taking hundreds, or even thousands of doses of LSD at once with little to no negative effects. (Other than a trippy time)

It's important to note that a psychedelic trip at any dose will affect your thought patterns. Even a good trip can lead you to question how you see yourself, your relationships with friends and family, and the world around you.

Keep in mind that the physical safety of the drug is only one side of the coin. Overdose is still a possibility with psychedelics like MDMA (E, X, Molly, Ecstasy) and ketamine (K, Special K). There have been deaths directly caused by doing too much in one night.

Often, especially with MDMA, pills are dosed at 2 to 3 times the safe, effective dose. Meaning that in some cases, when people buy pressed powder pills of MDMA, they can be sold a pill that can be way stronger than they wanted. And this can lead to negative experiences, and if the users are not careful, death. But a 2009 study showed that you are more likely to die while riding a horse than by taking MDMA, or ecstacy.

When moving around a lot on MDMA, it's important to stay hydrated. The combination of body heat from things like dancing, combined with MDMA has caused cases of overheating, and even death in some cases.

With drugs such as Ketamine, it's always best to test your substance, because who is to know what is really in that off-white powder? It's impossible to tell what the contents of powdered drugs are without testing them with reagent kits.

Deaths can sometimes be caused by using a different drug by accident, or by using something that was contaminated with a more dangerous drug, like fentanyl which is impossible to detect without using a test kit for your drugs.
This is also a danger for those who use LSD. Research

chemicals like 25i-Nbome are sometimes sold as "acid", and can be deadly in the same dose range. This can lead the user to believe that what they bought was LSD, and that it would be safe to do a large dose.

For example, travelling to another country for a psychedelic experience has its own risks. How reputable is the facility you plan to go? Do you trust the person guiding you, even though you may have just met? How much money are they asking for? How likely are you to get sick in some way from travelling?

But dear reader, you and I both know that people are going to use drugs. People will seek to alter their minds until the end of human history. After all, We've been using one drug or another since the dawn of recorded history, if not earlier. So why stop now? Let's keep each other safe instead.

The Final thing to remember, is to avoid mixing psychedelic drugs with medication. Psychedelics like LSD, and MDMA, can cause something called Serotonin Syndrome. This only happens when taken regularly at high doses. For example, if you took a heroic dose of LSD every week for the next six months.

Serotonin Syndrome will most likely not occur if you take a psychedelic drug once, or if you took a few doses over a week at an ayahuasca retreat. It only really happens if you combine antidepressant, anti-anxiety, and antipsychotic medications with extended periods of heavy psychedelic use.

Psychedelics may also awaken underlying mental health issues, such as schizophrenia if there is a history of these illnesses in your family. This is why it's best to avoid psychedelic drugs entirely if you have a risk of schizophrenia, depersonalization disorder, or if you simply have trouble coping with reality. These substances have the chance to alter the way you see the world. So it's important to be careful when considering taking any substance.

It's recommended that you try alternative forms of consciousness exploration if you are at a risk of mental illness. These can include meditation, lucid dreaming, holotropic breathwork, yoga, or other mindfulness practices. Psychedelics may launch people into an altered state of mind, but it's perfectly possible to reach the same altered state by not ingesting any drugs whatsoever. Your body is, and will always be hard wired for a spiritual type-experience.

# Smoked Cannabis
## (Weed, Marijuana, Ganja)

## Safety Info

Cannabis is one of the most widely used drugs on earth. Humans have been farming weed for thousands of years. It was historically used for medicine, industrial use, and as an intoxicant. When smoking or vaporizing cannabis it can last 1 to 4 hours This will depend on how high of a tolerance you have to cannabis. People who smoke more will have a higher tolerence for cannabis will experience effects for a shorter time than those who have a low tolerance. Effects will escalate quickly, within 2 to 5 minutes.

## Duration of Effects

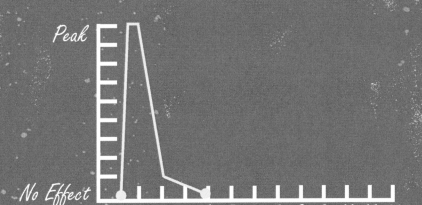

Length (Hours)

## Duration of effects (continued)

| | |
|---|---|
| Total time: | 1 to 4 hours |
| Onset: | 0 to 10 minutes |
| Come up: | 5 to 10 minutes |
| Plateau: | 15 to 30 inutes |
| Come down: | 45 to 180 minutes |
| After effects: | 2 to 24 hours |

## Dose

Dosing will depend on several factors (see the intro to this section). But here are genral guidlines based on the chemistry of cannabis. Keep in mind, regular users may have a higher tolerance and may need more to experience the same effects.

Effects are noticed at: 0.3 to 0.5 grams

Light dose: 0.75 to 1 gram

Standard dose: 2 to 3.5 grams

Heavy dose: 4 or more grams

# Edible Cannabis
## (Food and Drinks)

## Safety Info

Cannabis edibles, like brownies, or tea can last 5 to 6 hours depending on how much you took. People with a higher tolerence for cannabis will feel effects for a shorter time than those who have a low tolerance. Effects will escalate much slower than smoking, and reach their most intenst point around 2 hours after ingesting.

## Duration of Effects

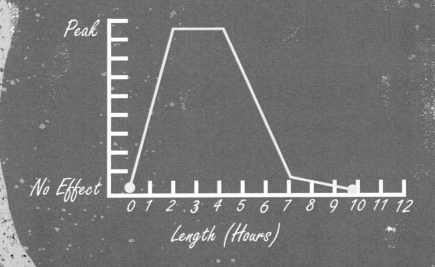

## Duration of effects (continued)

| | |
|---|---|
| Total time: | 4 to 10 hours |
| Onset: | 30 to 120 minutes |
| Come up: | 30 to 60 minutes |
| Plateau: | 2 to 5 hours |
| Come down: | 1 to 2 hours |
| After effects: | 6 to 24 hours |

## Dose

Cannabis edibles can be very slow to take effect, and can often feel much stronger than smoking. It's best to start with a low dose and wait about 40 minutes to see if you want to take a booster dose.

Effects are noticed at: 10 to 20 micrograms (ug)

Light dose: 20 to 75 micrograms (ug)

Standard dose: 100 to 150 micrograms (ug)

Heavy dose: 150 micrograms (ug) and up

## List of possible effects

The effects listed here aply to both smoked and edible cannabis. While the duration of edible versus smoked cannabis is different, the effects that it produces are nearly identical, with edible cannabis being the more intense of the two experiences.

### Positive

- Mood lift, euphoria
- Increased giggling and laughing
- Relaxation, stress reduction
- Creative, philosophical, abstract, or deep thinking
- Change in experience of muscle fatigue
- Pleasant body feelings
- Increase in connection to mind, and body
- Pain relief (headaches, muscle-pain, cramps)
- Reduced nausea, increased appetite
- Reduced neuropathic pain and spasticity due to multiple sclerosis
- Reduced seizure frequency / increases 'seizure threshold' in sensitive individuals
- Increased appreciation or awareness of music; deeper connection to music; increased emotional impact of music
- Increased awareness of senses (taste, smell, touch, hearing, vision)

### Neutral

- General change in consciousness
- Change in vision, such as sharpened colors or lights
- Closed-eye visuals (somewhat uncommon)
- Tiredness, sleepiness, lethargy
- Stimulation, inability to sleep (less common)
- Dry or sticky mouth
- Difficulty following a train of thought

- 🍁 Racing thoughts (especially at high doses)
- 🍁 Altered sense of time
- 🍁 Increased appetite, AKA "the munchies"
slowness (slow driving, talking)
- 🍁 Blood-shot eyes (more common with certain strains of cannabis and inexperienced users)

## *Negative*

- 🍁 Coughing
- 🍁 Can irritate asthma, and upper respiratory problems
- 🍁 Difficulty with short-term memory
- 🍁 Racing heart, agitation, feeling tense
- 🍁 Mild to severe anxiety
- 🍁 Headaches (at higher doses)
- 🍁 Paranoid nd anxious thoughts
- 🍁 Possible psychological dependence on cannabis
- 🍁 Clumsiness, loss of coordination at high doses
- 🍁 Nausea, especially in combination with alcohol, some pharmaceuticals, or other drugs
- 🍁 Panic attacks in sensitive users or with very high doses (oral use increases risk of getting too much)
- 🍁 Dizziness, confusion, lightheadedness or fainting (in cases of lowered blood pressure)

(12) Cannabis flowers, or buds.
(strain: Snoop's Dream)

(13) Cannabis edibles,
(Courtesy of Heavenly High.)

# Psilocybin
## (magic mushrooms)

### Safety Info

Psilocybin mushrooms are among the safest drugs on earth. They last about 6 to 9 hours. Lighter doses will typically end sooner than larger doses. The effects reach their peak intensity after one hour. Psilocybin is reknown for it's ability to "reset" the brains of people with mental illnesses like PTSD and addiction. It is currently being used to treat end-of-life anxiety in cancer patients, and has become a "breakthough" for mental health treatment.

### Duration of Effects

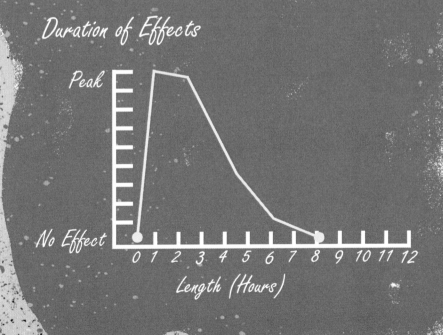

## Duration of effects (continued)

| | |
|---|---|
| Total time: | 6 to 9 hours |
| Onset: | 20 to 60 minutes |
| Come up: | 15 to 30 minutes |
| Plateau: | 3 to 6 hours |
| Come down: | 3 to 5 hours |
| After effects: | 2 to 5 hours |

## Dose

Psilocybin mushrooms are dosed by the dry gram, and not by the number of mushrooms. "Strains" of different psilocybe cubensis mushrooms have no noticable differences in psilocybin content. Different species of mushroom however, may be more or less potent depending on the species. For example are the most potent in the world, with around 2% content. Psilocybe cubensis, the species most commonly used, has between half a percent to one percent psilocybin content.

| | |
|---|---|
| Effects are noticed at: | 0.3 to 0.5 grams |
| Light dose: | 0.75 to 1 gram |
| Standard dose: | 2 to 3.5 grams |
| Heavy dose: | 4+ grams |

## List of possible effects

The effects listed here may not apply to the experience you had. instead it covers a basic list of the general effects experienced while on psilocybin.

### Positive

- Mood lift, euphoria
- Increased giggling and laughing
- Creative, philosophical or deep thinking
- Ideas flow more easily
- Sensation of insight
- Life-changing spiritual experience
- Intense feelings of wonder
- Boring tasks or entertainment can become more interesting or funny

### Neutral

- Feeling more emotionally sensitive
- Lights and colours seem brighter
- Star and rainbow patterns around pinpoint lights
- Increased detection of motion in peripheral vision
- Sleepiness, lethargy
- Pupil dilation
- Sensation of energy or buzzing in the body
- Memories become very vivid
- Open and closed-eye visuals (common at medium or stronger dose)
- General change in consciousness (as with many psychoactives)
- Time seems to pass more slowly (minutes seem to take hours)

## *Negative*

- 🍄 Intense feelings of fear
- 🍄 Mild to severe anxiety
- 🍄 Confusion
- 🍄 Dizziness, vertigo
- 🍄 Problems remembering things
- 🍄 Headache, usually as effects wear off, sometimes beginning the next day, lasting for up to 24 hours
- 🍄 Nausea, gas, gastrointestinal discomfort, especially when mushrooms are eaten raw and/or dry
- 🍄 Feeling light-headed, fainting (in cases of lowered blood pressure)
- 🍄 Can precipitate or exacerbate latent or existing mental disorders

(10) Several grams of dried psilocybin mushrooms.

# LSD
## Lysergic Acid Diethylamide

### Safety Info

LSD, or acid, is most famous for it's role in the hippie and beatnick cultures of the 20th century. LSD lasts about eight to 12 hours. Smaller doses will usually end sooner than larger doses. Effects reach their peak after an hour. Always test LSD using the Ehrlich reagent test kit. Different names are given to different batches of LSD. These are just flashy, and tell you nothing about potency, or if it's real LSD. If you buy LSD, ask what the dose is on one tablet, or blotter. The myth of "bad acid" most likely comes from people using another drug on a blotter paper under the impression it was LSD. Or from accidentally using a tablet that was dosed with far too much LSD

### Duration of Effects

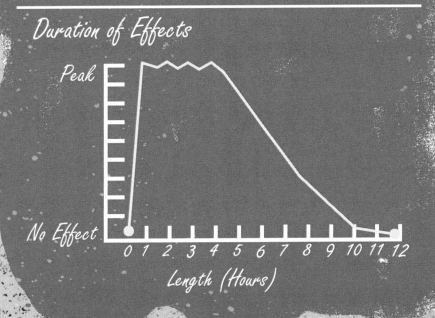

Length (Hours)

## Duration of effects (continued)

| | |
|---|---|
| Total time: | 6 to 12 hours |
| Onset: | 20 to 60 minutes |
| Come up: | 15 to 30 minutes |
| Plateau: | 3 to 6 hours |
| Come down: | 3 to 5 hours |
| After effects: | 2 to 5 hours |

## Dose

It's important to note that it's not possible to tell how much LSD is on a given tablet unless it's tested in a laboratory. So start with a low dose and wait about 40 minutes to see if you want to take a booster dose.

| | |
|---|---|
| Effects are noticed at: | 10 to 20 micrograms (ug) |
| Light dose: | 20 to 75 micrograms (ug) |
| Standard dose: | 100 to 150 micrograms (ug) |
| Heavy dose: | 150+ micrograms (ug) |

## List of possible effects

The effects listed here may not apply to the experience you had. instead it covers a basic list of the general effects experienced while on LSD.

### Positive

- Mental and physical stimulation
- Increase in associative & creative thinking
- Mood lift, euphoria
- Increased awareness & appreciation of music
- Sensory enhancement (taste, smell, sounds, etc)
- Therapeutic psychological reflection
- Feeling of being connected to the universe
- Blurring of boundaries between yourself and others
- Perspective, opinion altering
- Closed and open-eye visuals, including trails, color shifts, brightening, and so on
- Profound life-changing spiritual experiences or personal revelations

### Neutral

- General change in consciousness
- Pupil dilation
- Difficulty focusing
- Unusual thoughts and speech
- Change in perception of time
- Slight increase in body temperature
- Slight increase in heart rate
- Increase in yawning (without being tired)
- Looping, recursive, out of control thinking
- Increased salivation and mucus production (can cause coughing)

🎲 Unusual body sensations, facial flushing, chills, goosebumps, etc.
🎲 Quickly changing emotions (happiness, fear, gidiness, anxiety, anger, joy, irritation)

## Negative

🎲 Anxiety, paranoia, fear, and panic
🎲 Tension, jaw tension
🎲 Increased perspiration
🎲 Delusional, fanciful thoughts and ideas taken as fact
🎲 Difficulty regulating body temperature
🎲 Nausea, dizziness
🎲 Confusion
🎲 Insomnia
🎲 Megalomania
🎲 Overstimulation from music and other noise
🎲 Unwanted and overwhelming feelings
🎲 Unwanted or unexpected life-changing spiritual experiences or personal revelations
🎲 PTSD-style flashbacks or vivid memories of unpleasant visions, memories, or thoughts

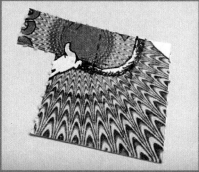

(11) Ten "tabs" of LSD on blotter paper.

# DMT
## Dimethyltriptamine

### Safety Info

DMT, or dimethyltriptamine, is the main ingredient in ayahuasca, a psychedelic tea traditionally used in the Amazon Rainforest by locals, and tourists alike. DMT has become popular in it's pure form because of its fast acting psychedelic effects when vaporized. Any dry herb vaporizer can be used. It can also be smoked in a regular pipe by placing it between two thicker layers on herb (any herb will do). DMT only lasts 20 minutes, and the peak (or flash) of the experience can be as short as 2 minutes, but can be longer as well. Because the effects are intense and immediate, you should be sitting down.

### Duration of Effects

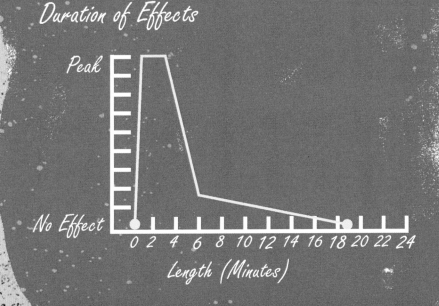

Peak

No Effect

0 2 4 6 8 10 12 14 16 18 20 22 24

Length (Minutes)

## Duration of effects (continued)

| | |
|---|---|
| Total time: | 5 to 20 minutes |
| Onset: | 0 to 1 minute |
| Come up: | 0 to 30 seconds |
| Plateau: | 3 to 15 minutes |
| Come down: | 3 to 5 minutes |
| After effects: | 15 to 60 minutes |

## Dose

Dosing will depend on several factors. But here are genral guidlines based on the chemistry of DMT. It can also be very harsh on the lungs when vaporized. DMT is often said to be difficult to vaporize because it can burn easily, and lose potency.

| | |
|---|---|
| Effects are noticed at: | 2 to 5 milligrams (mg) |
| Light dose: | 10 to 20 milligrams (mg) |
| Standard dose: | 20 to 40 milligrams (mg) |
| Heavy dose: | 40 to 60+ milligrams (mg) |

## List of possible effects

The effects listed here may not apply to the experience you had. instead it covers a basic list of the general effects experienced after vaporizing DMT. It is not uncommon for users of DMT to report speaking to spirits, dead relatives, and religious figures or telepathically communicating with other beings that are percieved during the experience. This is why many people seek out DMT, in order to enduce a kind of spiritual journey.

### Positive

- Short duration
- Spiritual experiences may occur
- Intense open eye visuals, kaleidoscopic patterns
- Feelings of insight
- Powerful "rushing" sensation
- Radical shift of opinions, perspective on life
- Profound, or meaningful experiences

### Neutral

- Change in perception
- Altered sense of time
- Auditory distortions and hallucinations (similar to buzzing, or the crackle of a flame)
- Visual distortions, and hallucinations (geometric patterns, landscapes, etc.)

## Negative

- ↻ Overly intense experiences can be hard to understand
- ↻ Harsh smoke/vapor on the lungs
- ↻ Fast onset and intensity can lead to problems if not prepared (dropped pipe, knocking things over, falling)
- ↻ Slight stomach discomfort
- ↻ Overwhelming negative emotions like fear, or panic

**(3) DMT** in a glass jar

# 5-MeO-DMT
## 5-Methoxy-Dimethyltriptamine

### Safety Info

5-MeO-DMT, is the psychoactive chemical in the venom of the Colorado River Toad (AKA the Senoran Desert Toad, or Bufo Alvarius). The toads have become an endagnered species. Habitat loss, and poaching are leading to the extinction of Bufo Alvarius. Lab-made synthetic 5-MeO-DMT gives users the exact same experience, without harming any toads or their habitats. So I ask that you do not seek out any toads, it's killing them. Any dry herb vaporizer can be used. It can also be smoked in a regular pipe by placing it between two thicker layers on herb (any herb will do).MeO-DMT can also be found in many plant species, or created in a lab. It lasts about same time as DMT, so you will begin to feel normal after 5 to 20 minutes. Sitting down is a must because of the speed, and how intense the effects are.

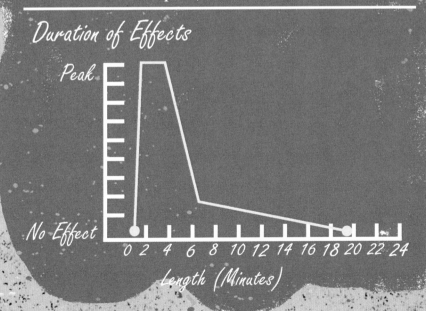

Duration of Effects

Peak

No Effect

0  2  4  6  8  10 12 14 16 18 20 22 24

Length (Minutes)

## Duration of effects (continued)

| | |
|---|---|
| Total time: | 5 to 20 minutes |
| Onset: | 0 to 1 minute |
| Come up: | 0 to 30 seconds |
| Plateau: | 3 to 15 minutes |
| Come down: | 3 to 5 minutes |
| After effects: | 15 to 60 minutes |

---

## Dose

Dosing will depend on several factors (see intro to this section). But here are genral guidlines based on the chemistry of 5-MeO-DMT. It can also be very harsh on the lungs when vaporized. 5-MeO-DMT is often said to be difficult to vaporize because it can burn easily. Don't put an open flame to it, you can end up destroying most of the dose.

| | |
|---|---|
| Effects are noticed at: | 1 to 2 milligrams (mg) |
| Light dose: | 2 to 5 milligrams (mg) |
| Standard dose: | 5 to 10 milligrams (mg) |
| Heavy dose: | 10 to 20+ milligrams (mg) |

---

## List of possible effects

The effects listed here may not apply to the experience you had. Instead it covers a basic list of the general effects experienced after vaporizing 5-MeO-DMT. Some people will choose to travel over-seas or out of their home country to have a guided 5-MeO-DMT, or "Toad" experience. Make sure you choose a reputable guide, or shaman, and be aware of the travel risks you will face, such as illness or injury.

### Positive

- Short duration
- Immersive experience or trip
- Powerful rushing sensation
- Radical perspective shifting
- Profound life-changing spiritual experiences
- Occasional euphoria
- Internal visions (actual visual effects not as common)

### Neutral

- Change in perception of time
- Experiencing "the void"
- Lack of memory of experience
- Muscle jerking, twitching, abnormal vocalizations
- Unconsciousness or non-responsiveness usually lasting 5-20 minutes, this is normal and to be expected.
- Dissociation from yourself or your body
- Increased salivation

## *Negative*

- Overly-intense experiences
- Hard on the lungs to smoke
- Increased salivation can become drooling at high doses
- Difficulty integrating experiences
- Feelings of fear, terror or panic (dysphoria)
- The fast onset and intensity can lead to some non-drug related issues when unprepared (dropping the pipe, knocking things over, falling down, hitting your head, etc.)

---

(4) Colorado River Toad, AKA Senoran Desert Toad (Incillius Alvarius, Bufo Alvarius).

# MDMA
## (Ecstacy, Molly)

### Safety Info

MDMA lasts 3 to 5 hours in total and can be felt after about 30 minutes. It's often sold under other names such as molly, mandy, M, and ecstacy. Keep in mind that pills of MDMA are often dosed higher than advertised. Your body weight plays a huge role in the dosing of MDMA, so take less if you weigh less. Make sure to test your MDMA with the Marquis reagent test kit whenever using. The list of effects provided covers the widest possible range of effects. It's best experience MDMA during a guided psychotherapy session if you can. But of course this will not be available to everyone. So if you are taking it, make sure to test your substance, and do it somewhere quiet, and calming. This way, you can avoid almost all of the risks involved.

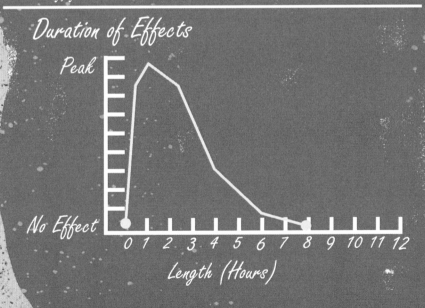

### Duration of Effects

Peak

No Effect

0 1 2 3 4 5 6 7 8 9 10 11 12

Length (Hours)

## Duration of effects (continued)

| | |
|---|---|
| Total time: | 3 to 5 hours |
| Onset: | 20 to 90 minutes |
| Come up: | 5 to 20 minutes |
| Plateau: | 2 to 3 hours |
| Come down: | 1 to 2 hours |
| After effects: | 2 to 24 hours |
| "Hangover": | 2 to 72 hours |

## Dose

Dosing will depend on several factors (see intro to this section) but MDMA is not like other drugs when it comes to dosing. Simply weighing out a dose is not enough to determine how much you need. The best way to tell what a normal or moderate dose of MDMA is for you involves some simple math...

1. Take your body weight, and divide it in half.
2. Take that number, and add 20 to it.
3. There you have your ideal moderate dose of MDMA, just for you!

So for example if you weigh 140 pounds, your moderate dose would be about 90 milligrams.
(ex: 140 pounds, divided by 2 = 70. 70+20= 90)

## Positive

- 🎲 Mild to extreme mood lift
- 🎲 Euphoria
- 🎲 Increased willingness to communicate
- 🎲 Increase in energy (stimulation)
- 🎲 Ego softening, ego dissolution
- 🎲 Decreased fear, anxiety, and insecurities
- 🎲 Feelings of comfort, belonging, and closeness to others
- 🎲 Feelings of love and empathy
- 🎲 Sense of peace and acceptance of self, others, and the world
- 🎲 Increased awareness & appreciation of music and art
- 🎲 Increased senses (taste, smell, sight, touch, hearing)
- 🎲 Life-changing spiritual experiences
- 🎲 Sensations bright and intense
- 🎲 Urge to hug and kiss people
- 🎲 Decreased pain perception

## Neutral

- 🎲 Decreased appetite
- 🎲 Increase in heart rate and blood pressure (dose related)
- 🎲 Strong desire to do more on the come-down
- 🎲 Decreased appetite
- 🎲 Visual distortion
- 🎲 Rapid, involuntary eye jiggling (nystagmus) mild visual hallucinations (uncommon)
- 🎲 Increased heart rate and blood pressure
- 🎲 Restlessness, nervousness, shaking
- 🎲 Change in body temperature regulation
- 🎲 Upwellings of unexpected emotion, emotional lability
- 🎲 Feeling of wanting to do or want more on the come down

## Negative

- 🎲 Inappropriate and/or unintended emotional bonding
- 🎲 Anxiety, agitation or paranoia (common)
- 🎲 Mild to extreme jaw clenching, tongue and cheek chewing, and teeth grinding

95

- 😈 Insomnia
- 😈 Short-term memory scramble or loss & confusion
- 😈 Short periods of disconnection from the external world (usually at very high doses or during brief blasts of intense rushing while coming up)
- 😈 Erectile disfunction and difficulty reaching orgasm
- 😈 Increased risk of overheating, or dehydration
- 😈 Hyponatremia (drinking too much water, while trying to stay hydrated)
- 😈 Nausea and vomiting, headaches, dizziness, loss of balance, and vertigo
- 😈 Sadness during come down, sense of loss or immediate nostalgia
- 😈 Post-trip crash - unpleasantly harsh comedown from the peak effect and hangover the next day, lasting days to weeks
- 😈 Mild depression and fatigue for up to a week, or severe depression and/or fatigue (uncommon)
- 😈 Possible psychotic episodes, severe panic attacks, etc requiring hospitalization (rare)
- 😈 Possible liver toxicity (rare) and possible neurotoxicity (controversial)
- 😈 Small risk of death; approximately 2 per 100,000 new users have extreme negative reactions resulting in death (rare)

(8) 100mg of pure MDMA powder

# Ketamine
## (K, Cat tranquilizer, Special K)

Ketamine is normally insufflated (snorted), and taken orally (in capsules or powder form). Nasal doses are very different than oral and intramuscular (IM) doses. A low dose nasally will be short and much different from the same dose taken orally. It is common to have muscle pain when injecting larger doses of Ketamine into the muscle. The pain can continue for several days if it's not injected properly. The muscle soreness can be somewhat controlled by using a very fine needle It should take 10-30 or more seconds to inject a dose into a muscle. If you feel it begin to sting, slow down the injection rate. IM and IV administration generally produce a higher peak, and a shorter overall duration than other methods. Doses are measured in milligrams (mg), and always use the Mandelin test kit before you use.

## Duration of effects

| | |
|---|---|
| Total time: | 30 to 60 minutes |
| Onset: | 5 to 10 minutes |
| Come up: | 10 to 30 minutes |
| Plateau: | 20 to 40 minutes |
| Come down: | 30 to 60 minutes |
| After effects: | 1 to 3 hours |
| "Hangover": | Possible |

## Dose

Ketamine can be a bit confusing to dose properly. This can lead some to use too much by accident and go into a "k-hole" where the experience is usually too intense, hard to remember, or conprehend. Oral ketamine will be dosed differently from injected, or insufflated (snorted) doses.

### Insufflated Ketamine

Threshold: 10 to 15 mg | Standard dose: 30 to 75 mg
Light dose: 15 to 30 mg | Heavy dose: 60 to 125 mg

The "K-hole": 100 to 250 mg and up

---

### Oral Ketamine

Threshold: 40 to 50 mg | Standard dose: 75 to 300 mg

Light dose: 50 to 100 mg | Heavy dose: 200 to 450 mg

The "K-hole": 500 mg and up

---

### Intramuscular (IM) Ketamine

Threshold: 10 to 15 mg | Standard dose: 30 to 75 mg
Light dose: 15 to 30 mg | Heavy dose: 60 to 125 mg

The "K-hole": 100 to 250 mg and up

## List of possible effects

Ketamine has the potential to cause more harm than most psychedelic drugs. It has many side effects worth mentioning, due to their severity. They are listed below, and continue on the following page. Make sure to always test your ketamine before using.

### Positive

- Euphoria
- Sense of calm
- Reduced or eliminated acute pain.
- Visual, dream-like, visionary, and/or hallucinatory ideations.

---

### Neutral

- Distortion or loss of sensory perception
- Closed- and open-eye visuals
- Dissociation of mind from body
- Numbness (analgesia)
- Loss of motor coordination
- Change in perception of time
- Increase in heart rate
- Slurred speech
- Confusion or disorientation
- Out-of-body experience (O.B.E.)
- Shifts in perception of reality
- "K-hole": intense mind-body dissociation, out-of-body experiences, highly realistic visuals
- Complete unconsciouness, sedation at high doses

---

## *Negative*

(Negative side effects increase with higher doses and frequent use)

- Risk of psychological dependency (addiction)
- Nasal discomfort upon insufflation
- Discomfort, pain or numbness at injection site (with IM)
- Severe confusion, disorganised thinking
- Paranoia and egocentrism (with regular use)
- Nausea, vomiting
- Visual, dream-like, visionary, or hallucinatory ideations
- Distortion or loss of sensory perception
- Susceptibility to accidents (from uncoordination and change in perception of body and time)
- Severe dissociation, depersonalisation
- Loss of consciousness (dangerous or fatal in wrong circumstances)
- Depression of heart rate and respiration (risk increases with increased dose or when combined with depressants)

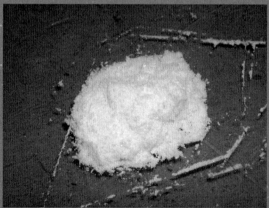

(9) Ketamine Hydrochloride.

# Set, Setting, and Intention

The words set, and setting are used a lot in the context of psychedelic drugs. The idea behind them is simple. The emotions you are feeling before a trip begins, and the people you are tripping with, will impact how your experience will go.

A psycheelic experience can be powerful and mind-changing. It can alter the way you see yourself and the world around you. This is why psychedelics should ideally be used in a controlled setting. These experiences do not always need to be guided by a doctor, or shaman. Many times, they can be done at home in the company of good friends or loved ones. Even alone, as long as someone knows what you're up to. Just in case of emergency.

## Set:

Set reffers to how you feel as you prepare for a psychedelic trip. Are you feeling energized? anxious? sad? happy? How you feel the day of your trip will always impact your emotions during the experience. If you're feeling angry about something for example, the trip may become more difficult to deal with because of outside emotional input. If you are feeling very relaxed, it may be easier to let yourself experience the trip.

## Setting:

Set reffers to where you are during your trip. The idea is to guage how much control you want over your environment during the trip. In other words, how unpredictable do you want the area to be? A loud concert will be more likely to provoke anxiety than your bedroom. This is not a hard and fast rule, but the more control you have over the disruptions in your immediate area, the better. Psychedelic trips are already highly unpredictable when it comes to the emotions you can experience. So, it's best to be in an area with less distruptions if you have little, or no experience with psychedelics.

## Intention:

Intention is the reason you are choosing to have a psychedelic experience. That being said, there is no wrong reason to take a psychedelic drug. Even taking a psychedelic just for fun is okay, as long as you understand how powerful, or emotional the experience can become.

It's best to not use these drugs just a way of "getting high". These are important and powerful drugs that can treat people suffering with mental illness, and alliviate a fear of death. Psychedelics can be used for any number of reasons, like treating depression, seeking a spiritual experience, wanting to be more in touch with nature, bonding with loved ones, as long as you know why you are taking it, you should get something good out of the experience. Some people have even used psychedelics to help them quit addictions like smoking cigarettes, or drinking.

# A Note to End on

"There are more things present in Heaven and Earth, Horatio, than are dreamt of in your philosophy," said the title character of William Shakespear's classic play "Hamlet".

What Shakespear meant to express in this quote was simple, "Open your mind, Horatio! The world does not revolve around your ideas," In other words, just because you don't understand something does not give you any authority over it.

For some illogical reason, we let law-makers decide what drugs are allowed to be used in our own private lives. This is an absolute disregard for the most basic of human rights, freedom. you have the right to control your own body, and yes this includes drug use, or at least it should.

Would you tell someone not to have sex? Would you tell someone that they couldn't eat dinner? Or eat a candy bar? Of course not! So, why would you tell someone that they are not allowed to have control over what happend to their mind? We let people drink alcohol, take pharmaceuticals, and smoke tobacco products all of which present serious health risks, so why not other drugs too?

The "War on Drugs" has not stopped, or even slowed down drug use. It has only made it easier to buy, sell, and use drugs. This backwards outlook on drug use has led to rampant rates of addiction, poverty, deaths, and overall suffering for the communities and people who continue to suffer from the effects of the drug war.

"Psychedelics are not illegal because a loving government is concerned that you'll jump out of a three story window. They are illegal because they dissolve opinion structures and culturally laid down models of behaviour and information processing. They [psychedelics] open you up to the possibility that everything you know is wrong," As ethnobotanist and author Terence McKenna said.

It's time to accept the science, this way we can change how we see drugs like LSD, MDMA, psilocybin mushrooms, and cannabis. Instead of giving people some kind of "high", these drugs have the potential to save lives, cure trauma, and cure mental illness.

The world is full of psychedelic drugs and plants that can help us reconnect to our history, to ourselves, and to the people around us. It's time we follow the example of ancient cultures, and find a way to use these psychedelics in a controlled, responsible way to help our communities grow and thrive.

Regardless of any laws, psychedelic drugs will continue to be taken by people across the globe. Psychedelic drugs continue to save lives, and stop suicide attempts. Psychedelic drugs have improved the quality of life for millions of people every year. No matter how illegal they became, no matter how many people were sent to death for using them, no matter how hard governments tried to stamp them out, psychedelics have always been with us. Psychedelic drugs have been with us since the dawn of humanity, and will be a part of the human experience until the very end.

# So in Conclusion...

## 1. You, have the right to alter your consciousness.

As a human being, you have the right to get high. Wether you choose meditation, lucid dreaming, alcohol or psychedelics. Nobody has the right to tell you what to do with your body. We need to remind ourselves that these plants, powders, pills and potions are normal, beautiful, healing, and deeply human experiences.

## 2. Test your drugs using a test kit.

If you can afford a drug, you can afford to test that drug using a reagent kit! Search for them online, using the information provided earlier in this book.

## 3. Different people, and places will change the trip.

Where you choose to have your psychedelic experience will impact the overall outcome. Being near plants, and nature or, somewhere you enjoy will make the trip more relaxing than being near strangers in an unfamilliar place.

## 4. Always have a sober person around.

It's best if you have someone sober nearby. This is often helpful when taking a psychedelic substance because they can help keep you calm if the experience bring up challenging emotions. You may not feel like this is needed, but it is. Even a night of drinking might require someone to be the designated driver.

## 5. Never "eye ball" your dose!
## Always use a Scale!

Always weigh out your dose! Jewelry scales can be purchased at many headshops, corner stores, or online. They are perfect for weighing out small amounts of drugs for personal use. It's impossible to "eyeball" the dose of any powdered drug. This is why every dose should be weighed out using a scale that can read milligrams (mg). Milligrams have three zeros behind the decimal point. (ex. 0.001)

## 6. On medication? Don't do psychedelics.

Serotonin Syndrome or Toxicity, is a risk when using psychedelics while on other medication. Doing a psychedelic at a normal dose occaisionally is not going to give you any life-threatening problems. It may dampen the effects, But Serotonin Toxicity, or S.T. for short, is not going to happen the as soon as you take the wrong mix of drugs. But it's still a risk, especially over long periods of using, or when taking unusually high doses. It's safer to simply not mix psychedelics with drugs such as antidepressant, anti-anxiety, and antipsychotics.

# Sources

## Introduction and Foreward:

1. World Health Organization (WHO), et al. "Global status report on alcohol and health 2018." who.int, 2018, https://www. who.int/substance_abuse/publications/global_alcohol_report/ en/. Accessed 10 October 2020.

2. Feuer, Will. "Oregon becomes first state to legalize magic mushrooms as more states ease drug laws in 'psychedelic renaissance.'" cnbc.com, CNBC News, 04 November 2020, https://www.cnbc.com/2020/11/04/oregon-becomes-first-state-to-legalize-magic-mushrooms-as-more-states-ease-drug-laws. html. Accessed 22 November 2020.

3. Snopes, and Madison Dapcevich. "Did Canada Approve Psychedelic Mushrooms for Depression and Anxiety Treatment?" Snopes, 18 November 2020, https://www.snopes.com/fact-check/ canada-psychedelic-depression/. Accessed 22 November 2020.

---

## The Stoned Ape:

1. Catlow, Briony J., and Shijie Song. "Effects of psilocybin on hippocampal neurogenesis and extinction of trace fear conditioning." Experimental Brain Research, vol. 228, 2013, pp. 481-491. National Center for Biotechnology Information, https:// pubmed.ncbi.nlm.nih.gov/23727882/. Accessed 31 October 2020.

2. Gimpl, M. P., et al. "Effects of LSD on learning as measured by classical conditioning of the rabbit nictitating membrane response." Journal of Pharmacology and Experimental Therapeutics, vol. 208, no. 2, 1979, pp. 330-334. National Center for Biotechnology Information, https://pubmed.ncbi.nlm.nih. gov/762668/. Accessed 31 October 2020.

3. Griffiths, Roland R., et al. "Psilocybin can occasion mystical-type experiences having substantial and sustained personal meaning and spiritual significance." Psychopharmacology, vol. 187, no. 3, 2006, pp. 268–83. Accessed 28 October 2020.

4. Stamets, Paul, and After Skool. "Stoned Ape & Fungal Intelligence - Paul Stamets." YouTube, After Skool - educational YouTube Channel, 13 March 2018, https://www.youtube.com/watch?v=Nxn2LlBJDl0&ab_channel=AfterSkool. Accessed 31 October 2020.

5. Stamets, Paul, and Fantastic Fungi - Film Website. "The Stoned Ape." Fantastic Fungi, 2020, https://fantasticfungi.com/the-mush-room/the-stoned-ape-theory/. Accessed 31 October 2020.

6. Wikimedia Foundation. ""Stoned Ape" Theory of Human Evolution." Wikipedia, 2020, https://en.wikipedia.org/wiki/Terence_McKenna#%22Stoned_ape%22_theory_of_human_evolution. Accessed 31 October 2020.

## The Philosopher's Stoned:

1. Muraresku, Brian. The Immortality Key: The Secret History of the Religion with No Name. Narrated by Brian Muraresku, forward narrated by Graham Hancock. Audible, 2020. Audiobook. Accessed 18 October 2020.

2. Barrett F.S., Griffiths R.R. (2017) Classic Hallucinogens and Mystical Experiences: Phenomenology and Neural Correlates. In: Halberstadt A.L., Vollenweider F.X., Nichols D.E. (eds) Behavioral Neurobiology of Psychedelic Drugs. Current Topics in Behavioral Neurosciences, vol 36. Springer, Berlin, Heidelberg. https://doi.org/10.1007/7854_2017_474. Accessed 28 October 2020.

3. Ruck, Carl A.P., et al. The Road to Eleusis: Unveiling the Secret of the Mysteries. 1st ed., Harcourt Brace Jovanovich, 1978. Accessed 31 October 2020.

4. Griffiths, Roland R., et al. "Psilocybin can occasion mystical-type experiences having substantial and sustained personal meaning and spiritual significance." Psychopharmacology, vol. 187, no. 3, 2006, pp. 268–83. Accessed 28 October 2020.

5. Grunwell, John N., and Multidisciplinary Association for Psychedelic Studies (MAPS). "Ayahuasca Tourism in South America." Newsletter of the Multidisciplinary Association for Psychedelic Studies, vol. 8, no. 3, 1998, pp. 59-62. Accessed 28 October 2020.

6. Horgan, John. "St. Anthony's Fire." Ancient History Encyclopedia, 17 July 2020, https://www.ancient.eu/St_Anthony's_Fire/#:~:text=X-,St.,the%20saint%20to%20do%20so. Accessed 25 October 2020.

7. Online Etymology Dictionary. "Pharmacy Etymology." Online Etymology Dictionary, https://www.etymonline.com/word/pharmacy. Accessed 26 October 2020.

8. Wikimedia Foundation. "Thyrsus, Staff." Wikipedia, 09 March 2020, https://en.wikipedia.org/wiki/Thyrsus. Accessed 25 October 2020.

9. Wikimedia Foundation. "Demeter at Eleusis." Wikipedia, 14 October 2020, https://en.wikipedia.org/wiki/Demeter#Demeter_at_Eleusis. Accessed 26 October 2020.
Wikimedia Foundation. "Persephone, The Eleusinian Mysteries." Wikipedia, 18 October 2020, https://en.wikipedia.org/wiki/Persephone#The_Eleusinian_mysteries. Accessed 25 October 2020.

## History of Cannabis:

1. Government of Canada. "Cannabis Market Data Overview." Canada.ca, 2020, https://www.canada.ca/en/health-canada/services/drugs-medication/cannabis/research-data/market.html. Accessed 28 October 2020.

2. Massachusetts Institute of Technology. "The People's History." The Thistle, vol. 13, no. 2, 2000, https://www.mit.edu/~thistle/v13/2/history.html#:~:text=Archaeologists%20found%20a%20remnant%20of,oldest%20example%20of%20human%20industry. Accessed 28 October 2020.

3. Ohlsson, A., et al. "Plasma delta-9-tetrahydrocannabinol concentrations and clinical effects after oral and intravenous administration and smoking." Clinical Pharmacology & Therapeutics, vol. 28, no. 3, 1980, pp. 409–416. American Society for Clinical Pharmacology and Therapeutics. Accessed 28 October 2020.

4. Ren, Meng, et al. "The origins of cannabis smoking: Chemical residue evidence from the first millennium BCE in the Pamirs." Science Advances, vol. 5, no. 6, 2019. ResearchGate, https://www.researchgate.net/publication/333734712_The_origins_of_cannabis_smoking_Chemical_residue_evidence_from_the_first_millennium_BCE_in_the_Pamirs. Accessed 28 October 2020.

5. Russo, Ethan B., et al. "Phytochemical and genetic analyses of ancient cannabis from Central Asia." Journal of Experimental Botany, vol. 59, no. 15, 2008, pp. 4171-4182. Oxford Academic, https://doi.org/10.1093/jxb/ern260. Accessed 28 October 2020.

6. Sayin, Umit. "The Consumption of Psychoactive Plants in Ancient Global and Anatolian Cultures During Religious Rituals: The Roots of the Eruption of Mythological Figures and Common Symbols in Religions and Myths." NeuroQuantology, vol. 12, no. 2, 2014, pp. 276-296. ResearchGate, https://www.researchgate.net/publication/269526783_The_Consumption_of_Psychoactive_Plants_in_Ancient_Global_and_Anatolian_Cultures_During_Religious_Rituals_The_Roots_of_the_Eruption_of_Mythological_Figures_and_Common_Symbols_in_Religions_and_Myths. Accessed 28 October 2020.

7. Wikimedia Foundation. "Coffeeshop (Netherlands)." Wikipedia, 2020, https://en.wikipedia.org/wiki/Coffeeshop_(Netherlands)#Coffeeshop_law. Accessed 28 October 2020.

Wikipedia. "Shennong." wikipedia.org, 9 October 2020, https://en.wikipedia.org/wiki/Shennong. Accessed 27 October 2020.

## Can Psychedelics be Medication:

1. Fadiman, James. "The Medical History of Psychedelic Drugs." A dissertation presented to The Department of History and Philosophy of Science, University of Cambridge, 2007. Accessed 28 October 2020.

2. Fadiman, James, and Sophia Korb. "Microdosing Psychedelics." microdosingpsychedelics.com, https://sites.google.com/view/microdosingpsychedelics/home. Accessed 24 October 2020.

3. Common Sense for Drug Policy. "Nixon Tapes Show Roots of Marijuana Prohibition: Misinformation, Culture Wars and Prejudice." CSDP Research Report, no. March, 2002, http://www.csdp.org/research/shafernixon.pdf. Accessed 29 October 2020.

4. Common Sense for Drug Policy. "Transcript of Nixon, Erlichman, Haldeman meeting." csdp.org, http://www.csdp.org/research/nixonpot.txt. Accessed 29 October 2020.

5. Petranker, Rotem, et al. "Psychedelic microdosing benefits and challenges: an empirical codebook." Harm Reduction Journal, vol. 16, no. 42, 2019, https://harmreductionjournal.biomedcentral.com/articles/10.1186/s12954-019-0308-4. Accessed 29 October 2020.

6. Science and Nonduality, and James Fadiman. "The Remarkable Results of Microdosing with James Fadiman." Science and Nonduality, Conference 2019, 23 October 2019, https://www.scienceandnonduality.com/video/the-remarkable-results-of-microdosing-james-fadiman. Accessed 31 October 2020.

# Mysteries of Egypt:

1. Berlant, Stephen R. "The entheomycological origin of Egyptian crowns and the esoteric underpinnings of Egyptian religion." Journal of Ethnopharmacology, vol. 102, no. 02, November 2005, pp. 275-288. Science Direct, https://www.sciencedirect.com/science/article/abs/pii/S0378874105005131?via%3Dihub. Accessed 28 December 2020.

2. Oliver-Bever, Bep. Medicinal Plants in Tropical West Africa. Cambridge University Press, 1986.

3. Russo, Ethan B. "History of Cannabis and Its Preparations in Saga, Science, and Sobriquet." Chemistry and Biodiversity, vol. 04, no. 08, August 2007, pp. 1614-1648. Wiley Online Library, https://onlinelibrary.wiley.com/doi/abs/10.1002/cbdv.200790144. Accessed 28 December 2012.

4. Wells, S.A. "American Drugs in Egyptian Mummies." Discoveries in Natural History & Exploration [University of California, Riverside.], https://faculty.ucr.edu/~legneref/ethnic/mummy.htm. Accessed 28 December 2020.

5. Wikimedia Foundation. "Hedjet." Wikipedia, 23 December 2020, https://en.wikipedia.org/wiki/Hedjet. Accessed 28 December 2020.

6. Wikimedia Foundation. "Hemhem Crown." Wikipedia, 07 August 2020, https://en.wikipedia.org/wiki/Hemhem_crown. Accessed 28 December 2020.

7. Wikimedia Foundation. "Hemp, cannabis, and medical cannabis in Egypt." Wikipedia, 05 April 2019, https://en.wikipedia.org/?title=Talk:Seshat#Hemp,_cannabis,_and_medical_cannabis_in_Egypt. Accessed 28 December 2020.

8. Wikimedia Foundation. "Henut Taui." Wikipedia, 15 November 2020, https://en.wikipedia.org/wiki/Henut_Taui. Accessed 28 December 2020.

## Rat Park:

1. Alexander, Bruce K., et al. "Effect of Early and Later Colony Housing on Oral Ingestion of Morphine in Rats." Pharmacology Biochemistry & Behavior, vol. 15, no. 4, 1981, pp. 571-576. Accessed 28 October 2020.
2. Hari, Johann, and TED Conferences. "Everything You Think You Know About Addiction is Wrong." TED Talks, June 2015, https://www.ted.com/talks/johann_hari_everything_you_think_you_know_about_addiction_is_wrong#. Accessed 29 October 2020.

---

## Testing and Weighing & What's a Reagent Kit:

1. Dance Safe. "Test Kit Shop." Dancesafe.org, 2020, https://dancesafe.org/shop/. Accessed 29 October 2020.
2. EZ Test Kits. "EZ Test Kit - Shop." eztestkit.com, 2020, https://www.eztestkits.com/en/ez-testing-kits. Accessed 29 October 2020.
3. Test Kit Plus. "Drug Identification Test Kits." Test Kit Plus - Shop, https://testkitplus.com/product-category/test-kits/drug-identification-test-kits. Accessed 29 October 2020.
4. DrugsData, and Erowid Center. "Fentanyl contamination in street drugs." drugsdata.org, 22 October 2020, https://www.drugsdata.org/results.php?search_field=all&s=fentanyl. Accessed 24 October 2020.
5. Hunt, Katie. "A woman took 550 times the usual dose of LSD, with surprisingly positive consequences." CNN, 29 February 2020, https://www.cnn.com/2020/02/27/health/lsd-overdoses-case-studies-wellness/index.html.

6. Nutt, David J., and University of Bristol. "Equasy –An overlooked addiction withimplications for the current debate ondrug harms." Journal of Psychopharmacology, vol. 23, no. 1, 2009, pp. 3-5. Research Gate, https://www.researchgate.net/publication/23806800_Equasy_-_An_overlooked_addiction_with_implications_for_the_current_debate_on_drug_harms. Accessed 04 January 2021.

## How to Stay Safe:

1. Erowid Center. "Cannabis." erowid.org, 27 May 2020, https://www.erowid.org/plants/cannabis/cannabis.shtml. Accessed 24 October 2020.
2. Erowid Center. "5-MeO-DMT." erowid.org, 19 October 2017, https://www.erowid.org/chemicals/5meo_dmt/5meo_dmt.shtml. Accessed 24 October 2020.
3. Erowid Center. "Ketamine." erowid.org, 08 March 2020, https://www.erowid.org/chemicals/ketamine/ketamine.shtml. Accessed 24 October 2020.
4. Erowid Center. "LSD-25." erowid.org, 17 July 2018, https://www.erowid.org/chemicals/lsd/lsd.shtml. Accessed 24 October 2020.
5. Erowid Center. "MDMA." erowid.org, 19 October 2017, https://erowid.org/chemicals/mdma/mdma.shtml. Accessed 24 October 2020.
6. Erowid Center. "N,N-DMT." erowid.org, 17 March 2018, https://www.erowid.org/chemicals/dmt/dmt.shtml. Accessed 24 October 2020.
7. Erowid Center. "Psilocybin Mushrooms." erowid.org, 28 May 2019, https://www.erowid.org/plants/mushrooms/. Accessed 24 October 2020.

8. Volpi-Abadie, Jacqueline, et al. "Serotonin Syndrome." The Ochsner Journal, vol. 13, no. 4, 2013, pp. 533-540. US National Library of Medicine National Institutes of Health, https://www. ncbi.nlm.nih.gov/pmc/articles/PMC3865832/. Accessed 01 November 2020.
9. Wikimedia Foundation. "Serotonin Syndrome." Wikipedia, 2020, https://en.wikipedia.org/wiki/Serotonin_ syndrome. Accessed 01 November 2020.

## Set, Setting, and Intention:

1. Wikimedia Foundation. "Set and Setting." Wikipedia, 12 September 2020, https://en.wikipedia.org/wiki/Set_and_setting. Accessed 24 October 2020.
2. Hartogsohn, Ido, and Multidisciplinary Association for Psychedelic Studies (MAPS). "The American Trip: Set, Setting, and Psychedelics in 20th Century Psychology." MAPS Bulletin Special Edition, vol. 23, no. 1, 2013, pp. 6-9. maps.org, https://maps.org/news/bulletin/articles/3549-special-edition-psychedelicspsychology. Accessed 01 November 2020.

## Clandestine Psychedelic Ceremonies:

1. Jesso, James W. Author, podcast host. Personal interview. 07 February 2020.
2. "Terry". Anonymous psychedelic user. Personal interview. 09 February 2020.
3. "Jack". Anonymous psychedelic user. Personal interview. 09 February 2020.
4. Global Drug Survey, and Adam R. Winstock. "GSD 2020: Psychedelics Under Supervision." Global Drug Survey, 2020, https://www.globaldrugsurvey.com/gds-2020/gds-2020-psychedelics-under-supervision/. Accessed 31 October 2020.
5. Global Drug Survey. "GSD 2020." Global Drug Survey 2020, 2020, https://www.globaldrugsurvey.com/gds-2020/. Accessed 31 October 2020.

# Photos:

1. Persephone, Demeter, and Triptolemos at Eleusis. (Courtesy Napoleon Vier. Nov, 30, 2005) (Title of photo: Eleusinian trio: Persephone, Triptolemos, and Demeter, on a marble bas-relief from Eleusis, 440–430 BC) (Link: https://commons.wikimedia.org/wiki/File:Eleusis2.jpg)

2. Ergot and Ergotism. 1931. Johns Hopkins University, Baltimore. WellComeCollection.org. Photograph. Accessed 28/10/2020.

3. DMT in a glass jar. January 2021. Own Work. Photograph. Accessed 11/01/2021.

4. Sonoran Desert Toad. Colorado River Toad. 27,October 2009. Secundum Naturam. Wikimedia Commons. Photograph. Accessed 29/10/2020.

5. Cannabis ready to harvest. October 2020. Own Work. Photograph. Accessed 29/10/2020.

6. Cannabis Nugs. October 2020. Own Work. Photograph. Accessed 29/10/2020.

7. Male Cannabis plant. July 2020. Own Work. Photograph. Accessed 29/10/2020.

8. 100mg of pure MDMA powder. January 2021. Own Work. Photograph. Accessed 11/01/2021.

9. Ketamine Hydrochloride. 4/20/2008. Coaster420. Own Work. Asia. Photograph accessed 11/01/2021.

10. (10) Several grams of dried psilocybin mushrooms. January 2021. Own Work. Photograph. Accessed 11/01/2021.

Manufactured by Amazon.ca
Bolton, ON

17662398R00071